Praise for

The New Commonsense Guide
to Your 401(k)

Rebuilding Your Portfolio from the Bottom Up

by Mary Rowland

"*The New Commonsense Guide* explains why 401(k) accounts remain a valuable component of our retirement plants, despite the market crash of 2008. And, it offers sound, highly-readable advice for managing them."

—MARK MILLER
Syndicated columnist, author of the forthcoming *The Hard Times Guide to Retirement Security*

"For most Americans, 401(k) plans are their last great hope for a secure retirement. Thankfully, one of the nation's top personal finance writers is on the case. Mary Rowland's *The New Commonsense Guide to Your 401(k)* will help you make the most of these sometimes daunting vehicles and get you on the path to a better financial future. You'll find this book to be time and money very well spent."

—DON PHILLIPS
Managing Director, Morningstar Inc.

"Mary Rowland's book is very timely and contains very useful information, regardless of your level of knowledge about investing and retirement planning."

—TED BENNA, "Father of the 401(k)"
Chief Operating Officer, Malvern Benefits

The New
COMMONSENSE
GUIDE TO YOUR
401(k)

Also available from
Bloomberg Press

Bonds:
The Unbeaten Path to Secure Investment Growth
by Hildy Richelson and Stan Richelson

Investing 101, Updated and Expanded
By Kathy Kristof

Investing in REITs:
Real Estate Investment Trusts
Third Edition
by Ralph L. Block

The Only Guide to Alternative Investments You'll Ever Need:
The Good, the Flawed, the Bad, and the Ugly
by Larry E. Swedroe and Jared Kizer

———————

A complete list of our titles is available at
www.bloomberg.com/books

The New COMMONSENSE GUIDE TO YOUR 401(k)

REBUILDING YOUR PORTFOLIO FROM THE BOTTOM UP

MARY ROWLAND

BLOOMBERG PRESS
NEW YORK

This publication contains the author's opinions and is designed to provide accurate and authoritative information. It is sold with the understanding that the author, publisher, and Bloomberg L.P. are not engaged in rendering legal, accounting, investment-planning, or other professional advice. The reader should seek the services of a qualified professional for such advice; the author, publisher, and Bloomberg L.P. cannot be held responsible for any loss incurred as a result of specific investments or planning decisions made by the reader.

Revised edition published 2010;
First edition published 1998
1 3 5 7 9 10 8 6 4 2

Library of Congress Cataloging-in-Publication Data

Rowland, Mary.
    The new commonsense guide to your 401(k): rebuilding your portfolio from the bottom up / Mary Rowland. -- Rev. ed.
        p. cm.
    Rev. ed. of: Commonsense guide to your 401(k). 1998.
    Includes bibliographical references and index.
    Summary: "The updated and expanded edition of the best step-by-step guide to investing in your 401(k) plan. Mary Rowland breaks down how 401(k) plans work, why they're still a smart investment, how to keep an eye out for hidden fees, and why now is the time to start reinvesting in your retirement"–Provided by publisher.
    ISBN 978-1-57660-327-7 (pbk.: alk. paper)
    1. 401(k) plans. 2. Pension trusts–United States. I. Rowland, Mary. Commonsense guide to your 401(k) II. Title.

HD7105.45.U6R68 2010
332.024#0145--dc22   2009046124

*To Mary Ann McGuigan, publisher,
fellow writer, and personal friend*

Contents

PART THREE: How to Get In and Get Out   85

PART FOUR: Investing   113

PART FIVE: Preparing for Change　173

PART SIX: Steps to Take in Retirement　203

The New COMMONSENSE GUIDE TO YOUR 401(k)

INTRODUCTION

When the stock market crashed on October 2, 2008, sending the Dow Jones Industrial Average down 348 points to 10,483, far from its high of 14,164.53 on October 9, 2007, a friend whom I'll call Susan said she felt happy to have all her money invested in a safe place where it wasn't affected by market turmoil. "I don't know how Bernard Madoff keeps producing these returns," she said then. "He's magic."

In January 2009, I met Susan, sixty, for coffee. She had lived a comfortable but not ostentatious life with the proceeds of her trust fund until she learned on December 11, 2008, that Madoff allegedly lost $51 billion of client money in a Ponzi scheme. "I'm a crook," Madoff told FBI agents. He claimed he worked alone to bilk investors, charities, banks, and other entities around the world. Since then, it's become clear that he had help. Susan lost her regular income plus the $5 million inheritance left by her father. She had about $6,000 in her checking account and no work experience.

Now she knows how Madoff produced magic: He recruited new investor money to send to earlier investors, pretending it was a return on their investment. To make his scheme work, he had to have a constant flow of fresh money to send to previous investors, claiming it was "income." Securities examiners say there is no evidence that Madoff invested or traded any of the $50 billion that he claims he collected in his Ponzi scheme. When the market began to sink at the end of 2007, Madoff investors began to ask for their money. By the fall of 2008 when banks, insurance companies, investment banks, auto companies began to fail and the world economy teetered on the verge of collapse, too many Madoff investors asked for a return of their principal. Madoff frantically tried to raise new money to return principal and pay returns to the investors who stayed, taking deposits as recently as nine days before his firm tanked. But by the end of

2008, it seemed that no one in America, or perhaps the world, had any money.

I realize it's difficult for many of us to feel compassion for someone who was once a millionaire. But Susan's father had instructed her to keep her money with Madoff, and told her that if she did so, she would be fine. In January, she told me that she never received her fourth-quarter payment from Madoff, and she didn't expect to receive another cent. Indeed, she feared that she would be asked to pay back some of the money. Susan had no job experience. She put her comfortable farmhouse on the market in what was a terrible real estate environment. But she was not having a pity party when I met her for lunch that day. Instead, she told me that she realized she hadn't really been alive until December 11 when she learned all her money was gone. Now she was determined to make her own way in the world.

For Susan and a number of other Madoff investors, the date of December 11, 2008, is seared into their minds just as September 11, 2001, is burned into all of our hearts. December 11 is the day Madoff investors got the phone call telling them that their money—all their money—was gone.

A sixty-year-old widow in suburban Philadelphia saw the $7.3 million she thought she had with Madoff disappear on the same December day.[1] Six days later, she was at work, caring for the ninety-three-year-old mother of a wealthy friend, returning items she'd recently bought with her credit card, and making plans to sell her Florida condo. A registered nurse, she planned to return to that profession.

Why am I telling you about these once-rich people? Because their lives fell apart just like the lives of many of the rest of us, only in some ways they have it worse, as they had no backup plan, no idea of how they would support themselves. Many Americans suffered the worst financial experience of a lifetime in 2008. Banks failed. Credit dried up. Mortgage rates increased, particularly for those who bought their homes with an initial "teaser rate" good for only a short period before dramatically ramping up. Household names like Merrill Lynch

---

1. Harold Brubaker, Philly.com, http://www.philly.com/philly/hp/news_update/20090122_West_Goshen_widow_s_riches-to-rags_story.html.

went down the tubes; Merrill itself was rescued only by a buyout by Bank of America, the largest U.S. bank, under pressure from the U.S. Treasury Secretary and Federal Reserve Chairman. Bank of America soon needed its own $20 billion government bailout. Citibank tottered toward destruction, saved only by a government bailout and the bank's agreement to break itself up into pieces. Businesses closed. By the end of the first quarter of 2009, five million workers had lost their jobs. Chrysler Corporation declared bankruptcy. And the Reserve Primary Fund, the first money market fund, created by Bruce Bent in 1972, "broke the buck," failing to hold the share price stable at $1. The stock market was down about 40 percent for 2008 and many investors lost more than 30 percent of their savings in 401(k) plans and other retirement investments.

So what kind of time is this to be publishing a book about 401(k) plans? A great time actually. Bloomberg published *A Commonsense Guide to Your 401(k)* in 1998, which provided a complete guide to retirement, including rules for getting in and out of 401(k) plans, investing the accumulated money, planning for a life both before and after retirement, as well as for reaching for your dreams and taking appropriate risks to achieve them rather than simply putting enough money aside to be able to feed yourself in later years while you sit on the couch and watch TV.

Perhaps our life goals seem uncertain now. But this is no time to give them up. As President Obama has said: Everything is possible. Anything is possible. We have many, many choices. We can choose to look backward at the crumbling of the financial structure and mourn or we can look ahead to a fresh start and determine that we will have the life we want.

The global financial crisis exposed myriad cracks in our financial safety net. Most of the cracks were already there. Some of us were operating on automatic pilot, stumbling from day to day to get the children off to school, get to work, come back home, and watch TV. Too many of us failed to focus on the things we'd hoped to achieve in our lifetime. We sidestepped our dreams because everyday living took all our energy. I see the 2008 financial collapse as an opportunity to help you, as an investor and as a person, take a fresh view of the way the investing world works, how it can work for you, and the amazing impact that can make on your life now as well as your life in retirement.

Already in 2008, 401(k) plan participants began to show more interest in saving for retirement, according to the report of Fidelity Investments on 2008 trends in 401(k) plans. Participants continued to contribute to their accounts in 2008, took fewer loans than in 2007, and improved asset diversification and decreased their holdings in company stock, all good signs. Fidelity received 100,000 calls a day from participants from late September through early October. On October 10, when the Dow Jones Industrial Average closed below 9,000 for the first time in five years, calls peaked at 120,000.

Lessons?

Most everyone in the United States today knows about the stock market crash of 1929 and the Great Depression of the 1930s. The collapse must have been earned, some Americans reason, by the excesses of the Jazz Age in the 1920s when investors sought cheap thrills, lighting cigars with ten-dollar bills and drinking champagne from glass slippers. Were these frenetic pleasure seekers in the jazz age real Americans? They were not like us—not practical and sensible and putting family first. They had money to burn. They burned it. And they got burned. The 1920s and the Great Depression seem almost like a morality play: Investors should have been punished for burning money rather than spreading it out to those in need.

The stock market crash of 1987 looked quite different. Here were the sons and daughters of the Great Depression babies, the hippies who belatedly got jobs and started families and, okay, maybe they were getting cocky about earning big salaries, living high on the hog. But after all, it was their own money. They earned it, and with the "invention" of 401(k) plans by R. Theodore Benna (Ted), who designed the first one to open January 1, 1981, the baby boomers had every reason to learn about investing and to win big in these retirement plans. Investors affected by the crash of 1987 were us: our parents, our neighbors. All of these other Americans who were working hard, trying to make it. Did they deserve this harsh punishment? As it turned out, the investors burned in the 1987 crash hardly remembered it.

The market rebounded so quickly that a decade later Americans were throwing everything they had into the market, borrowing money to buy stocks, day trading at the office, garnering bragging rights to show off at the Friday night cocktail hour.

When the tech bubble burst in March 2000, few of us could say that the market crash was someone else's fault. Most of us were caught up in it. Too many saw the stock market as a giant slot machine that spouted money no matter what you put in it, too many had stretched too far and were feeling giddy about the easy money to be made in day trading—truckers and caterers and teachers and all our other friends. Still, in the back of our minds we knew that we'd been warned. We knew that we'd been foolhardy. Time to suck it up and play the game conservatively. And how long did that last? The NASDAQ Index hit a high of 5,048 on March 10, 2000, and dropped to 1,114 on October 9, 2002.

So shouldn't we have seen it coming this time? What excuse do we have for 2008? Wall Street excesses? That contributed to the problem, sure, all the Wall Street firms and banks across the country that leveraged their balance sheets to load on risky debt. But individual excess contributed too. Why did all of us Americans continue to buy houses even as the housing market soared out of sight, when standard, three-bedroom, split-level homes were selling for more than half a million dollars? We should have known that the bubble had moved from tech stocks to real estate. In 2008, nobody was lighting his cigar with a ten-dollar bill. But lots of us were unrealistic and greedy.

This time there was no safe haven. And investors had no one to blame. It's easy to say that the other guy didn't keep his promises. But saying so didn't save any investments this time. Plenty of us happily participated in blowing this giant bubble. Students watched promised college aid packages go up in smoke. Colleges saw their operating funds frozen so they couldn't get the money they needed for day-to-day expenses. What should we have done differently? We shouldn't have borrowed so much. We shouldn't have leveraged so much. We should have been more careful. We should have kept informed. Next time we'd better be informed. It's time to stop looking back and asking ourselves whose fault it is. Who can we sue? How can we avoid taking responsibility for the fact that we lost our investments and savings? Of course, many investors were careful, saving prudently and investing conservatively. This time the markets surprised even professional investors.

Save Us from Ourselves

Make no mistake about this one: we are all in it together. Sure, we can blame Congress for failing to save this or that company or banks for leaving distressed homeowners holding the bag for a home that's worth less than the mortgage to pay it off. Or we can blame advisors who urged us to get into the market. This is the same refrain we've been hearing since the 1970s: Why has my employer "downsized" me? Or "rightsized" me? Why have I lost my defined benefit plan? Why do I have to pay more for my own health care? Why am I the victim? Who can I sue? In 2008, everybody was a loser. Big pension funds and endowment funds—even at Harvard and Yale—sank dramatically in value. No one knew how to protect himself from the financial hail storm that ended 2008. The experts were no better off than you were. So let's dust ourselves off and move forward.

The right questions to ask are the following: *How can I better take care of myself in a quickly changing world? How can I create the career I want, always willing to adjust as I learn more and gain experience? How can I live where I want to live? Learn more? Explore my passions?* You could never count on a big corporation to do these things for you. You could never count on the government to do these things for you. Resting in someone else's large hands might mean you are protected to continue doing what they want you to do. It never meant you were free to do what you wanted to do.

Ten years ago, I wrote a book about 401(k) plans with great expectations. I hoped it would help readers squeeze the most value from their 401(k) plans, certainly. But the book had the ambition of going beyond that: it aimed to help you to think about how to use your capital to create the life you want for yourself along the way, as well as in retirement.

Back then, corporate America was restructuring radically, and many Americans were not included in the new plan. We'd experienced a booming stock market for eight years. Some investors were sitting on a pile of gains and feeling smug. But the story of the economic expansion certainly had not been one of prosperity for all Americans. The expansion masked a lot of pain. Thousands of workers felt that this period of economic growth was built on their broken backs. Behind the story of growth was the story of the severed employment contract. Gone was the promise that if you work hard, your employer will take care of you both as a worker and as a retiree. And that was a decade ago!

Rich for Life

Rich is subjective. The 401(k) plan is a small but important tool for you to use; what you do with it depends on whether you view this glass as half empty or half full. To move toward independence, you must do some serious thinking about where you are going in your career and in your life and how your 401(k) plan might help you get there. Let's start with why the 401(k) plan was developed, where it came from, why it has grown, and how it works. Then we'll explore what that can mean for you both today and later in your nonworking years. In other words, rather than looking at your life divided into two parts—work and retirement—think of what you want to get out of it as a whole and start moving!

The massive corporate restructurings of the last two decades of the twentieth century probably seem like cruel punishment to some of the millions of people who were forced out of work and into lesser jobs. A growing chunk of the workforce is now employed as temporary or contract workers. These people have no employee benefits, which makes them a much cheaper source of labor for employers. They provide a vast pool of "just-in-time labor," holding down wages for others who do hold jobs. Of course, not all of these contract workers are unhappy with their jobs. Many see self-employment as freedom and wonder why it took them so long to find this life. Freedom is also subjective.

I once thought of freedom as defined by the Murray N. Burns character played by Jason Robards in the movie *A Thousand Clowns*. The clowns are the rest of us, the nondescript folks who tramp the streets of Manhattan or Chicago or Minneapolis on our way to work each morning at an insurance brokerage, ad agency, department store, bakery. Meanwhile, Robards' character looks out his window and laughs at the mindless clowns who work for a living while he plans his latest ruse to trick someone into paying him for loafing.

Moviegoers in the late 1960s cherished this movie. Freedom looked to be the only possible answer—the freedom to sing or paint or write or run through the park or sit in a coffee house and chat about existentialism. To the baby boomers, freedom meant going to rock concerts or debating anarchy versus nihilism or watching the Beatles' film *The Yellow Submarine*.

But look what happened to us freedom lovers: we began to weigh the value of what we thought of as freedom versus the freedom to buy a house and have a family. For most of us, the traditional life won out. We went back to school, became corporate lawyers and investment bankers and professors. We flung ourselves into our new bourgeois lives, earned a good deal of money, bought expensive houses and jewelry and vacations, imported European baby cribs and chocolates. It seemed that if we were going to work, we deserved the best. We'd given up our freedom after all.

But expensive does not equate with value, as the baby boomers soon learned. I met a man at my husband's high school class reunion who told me he was "a poet stuck in a lawyer's body." When I talk to financial advisors, they tell me most of their clients have enough money. What most of them can't seem to find is the magic potion that brings satisfaction or fullness to a life. So once again, we're looking for freedom.

One thing that I've learned in thirty years of writing about money is that the decisions people make are usually based on emotions rather than dollars and sense—that the unhappiness surrounding money comes not from how much money is available but how it is used. Most Americans fail to achieve what they could in life and fall short of realizing their dreams, not for lack of money but because they don't understand what they want their money to buy.

I once believed money might buy me the freedom to watch out the window while the clowns trekked to work. What I found is that money more often becomes an albatross. Getting married, buying a home, having or adopting a child, changing careers. Too often life passages bring not joy but a startling loss of freedom. Not the elusive potion that leads to happiness but more responsibilities, a tighter noose. So that we are left saying: "I have to buy this expensive piece of jewelry or take this expensive vacation because I deserve it, because I've worked so hard. Because I've lost my freedom." But what we really want is more balance in our lives.

So at the same time that I urge you to pay attention to your 401(k) plan and to squeeze it for all it's worth, I suggest that you take a look at the trajectory of your life, where it's going, where it's been. We all hear about people who are disappointed in retirement, depressed and regretful. The time to think about avoiding that is way before you get to retirement. I do a lot of work with financial advisors. Over the past decade, they have been telling me that what they see most often in affluent clients is that they feel they've sold their integrity or their dreams for a dollar.

Happily, financial advisors have responded to this search for value, for integrity, in their clients. Many of them have turned to what they call "life planning," by which they mean helping a client identify the passion in his life and then using his money to achieve it. Whether or not we use a financial planner, I think all of us should be looking at life planning rather than just planning to have enough dollars to eke out a paltry existence during retirement.

The planner who is generally given credit as the father of the life-planning movement is George Kinder, Harvard graduate, certified public accountant, bon vivant. "I think too much emphasis is placed on retirement planning to the exclusion of creating a happy life for yourself," says Kinder, who is also a Buddhist teacher.

Some years ago, Kinder took the Hawaiian vacation he had always dreamed about. Maui was everything he had expected and more. He discovered a different side of himself that he hadn't known existed in his buttoned-down life of the mind in Cambridge, Massachusetts. Spending more time in Hawaii became a top financial-planning goal and he stretched out his annual vacations to three and then four weeks. Still unsatisfied, he set up a financial-planning practice in Maui and began spending six months of the year there and six in Cambridge.

Kinder didn't stop there. He went on to sell his financial planning practice and set up the Kinder Institute for Life Planning where he offers workshops to help advisors work on life planning with their clients.

I attended one of the workshops in the summer of 2008. I was so inspired that I felt everyone should be able to use these life exercises.

Kinder is perhaps best known for the "three questions" he recommends each person ask himself: "How would you live your life if you had all the money you needed? What would you do if you learned you had only five to ten years to live? What would you most regret if you had just twenty-four hours left?" In our workshop, after we'd written out answers to these questions, we went on to learn about what brings us anxiety and what brings us joy in our own experiences with money.

Although most participants—there were about twenty to thirty total—were financial planners, some from independent firms or large multi-family offices like GenSpring, others from small community banks or large global banks, each of us participated in the workshop as a personal experience first, one that opened our eyes to money disorders in our own lives. This made clear how crucial the preliminary step is to understand and clear away the obstacles before turning to the dollars and cents of planning.

We worked with partners, exploring how early money experiences shaped us or singed us. For example, Kinder had each member of the twosome practice telling a personal money story to the partner. The partner was not allowed to say anything during the story. Listening is a crucial part of what Kinder teaches. He cites a study that claims the time between the advisor's first question to the client: "Why are you here?" and the beginning of sales pitch about a product is eighty-two seconds on average. Not much time to get a flavor of the client's life. Listening proves critical.

One of the most impressive parts of Kinder's presentation is his focus on integrity, honesty, and personal freedom. He calls on us to act with integrity, from a place of wholeness and clarity, in regard to personal values. He urges us to "identify and face the places where you lack integrity regarding money and clean them up." Whether we believe money is fair at its base or unfair at its base, Kinder says, if we cling to one side and see all of life through that lens, we are trapped, excluded from adulthood, unable to achieve all we could in life.

He talks about the patterns of "resent, blame, and complain," which are more familiar to most of us than clarity and integrity around money. Who hasn't had a friend who can't move off the idea that Dad didn't leave him enough money and life is unfair, and that if only he'd received the inheritance, if only he'd been promoted on the job, if only his wife hadn't turned out to be such a spendthrift, things would be perfect now.

This is not a self-help book. I'm not going to talk about the power of positive thinking or scold you about debt or lecture you about paying yourself first. Still, I can't resist urging you to make the most of the tools that are available to you in order to improve your life. Inasmuch as you can view the revolution in the American workplace as an opportunity for you to create independence for yourself rather than seeing it as a cause for disappointment, you will certainly have a better work life and a better retirement life. The 401(k) plan can play a key role in helping you to do that.

In the Beginning

To understand the role this plan plays in modern corporate American, it's helpful to take a look at its roots, which are to be found in this very same restructuring, in the plans of corporations to reduce their responsibility for employee benefits like pensions and health care coverage and other perks. It is a fascinating story of how one person helped shape the most vital savings tool many Americans have today.

Congress added paragraph k to section 401 of the Internal Revenue Code as part of the Revenue Act of 1978. But that paragraph might have gone unnoticed. Paragraph k simply permitted companies to set up tax-deferred savings plans so long as the plans didn't unduly favor the top-earning one-third of the company's employees. In other words, it provided for a "discrimination test." If an employee benefit is to receive a tax advantage, it must be offered (and used by) employees at various income levels. It may not unfairly advantage those employees in the higher ranks of the company, who are higher paid. This paragraph said that deferred savings plans must pass that test—nothing too remarkable about that.

There was a reason for addressing this issue in the tax bill, though. Paragraph k was actually written to resolve a conflict over cash profit-sharing plans that were prevalent among major companies in the early 1970s. Many companies had replaced year-end cash bonuses with plans that allowed employees to set aside a portion of the bonus in a tax-deferred account.

Tax deferral is always more appealing to those who make more money and pay more tax. (At the time, we had a series of different tax rates that peaked out at 70 percent.) Lower-paid workers are less likely to opt for tax deferral. They pay less tax and they have less money to stretch to meet their needs. Suppose a bank teller typically received an $800 bonus at Christmas time. Under the bank profit-sharing plans of the early 1970s, half of that would go into the retirement plan, and the teller could choose whether to defer the other half as well or to take that $400 in cash. This hybrid plan also typically allowed employees to withdraw money from the retirement plan after two years.

Although all workers had the same options, they didn't make the same choices. The higher-paid workers chose to defer their entire bonus while lower-paid workers typically chose half cash and then pulled the rest of the money out of the plan as soon as possible. The government objected to this arrangement because the tax benefit was really going to higher-paid employees who could afford to defer the income and get the advantage of pre-tax buildup of principal. The fact that everyone had the same opportunity was immaterial from the government's point of view because everyone did *not* get the same advantage from the tax deferral.

In 1972, the Internal Revenue Service ruled that no new hybrid bonus plans like these could be set up. Two years later, the Employee Retirement Income Security Act (ERISA), was passed. ERISA was landmark legislation, providing a massive body of rules and regulations to govern private pension plans and to protect the participants in them.

When ERISA was passed, Congress said that it would make a ruling on the hybrid plans. That happened in 1978 when paragraph k was written, stipulating that the plans could continue but only if the didn't favor the top one-third of employees. Paragraph k took effect in January 1980.

Like other benefits consultants, Ted Benna read paragraph k carefully. Even though it presented nothing really new, employee benefits consultants serve their clients by giving them opportunities to use government rules to make their benefits efficient and cost effective.

"The myth was that nobody knew it was there," Benna says. "But that wasn't true. I studied it and so did anyone else who follows this section of the law." But no one saw it as particularly significant. "January came and went and nobody was doing anything," Benna said. But he didn't drop it. He was working with a bank that wanted to revamp its traditional defined benefit pension plan and eliminate an old cash bonus plan. (Defined benefit plans get their name because the plan "defines" the benefit you will receive in retirement, based on your years of service, your salary and so forth. Funding the plan and paying out the benefit are the responsibilities of the employer.)

It was clear to Benna that section 401's paragraph k would permit his bank client to replace the cash bonus plan with a deferred profit-sharing plan, provided the new plan included lower-paid workers so that it would meet the discrimination test. But Benna didn't think lower-paid workers would participate. Why should they set aside part of their salary for later when they needed every penny right now? If they did not participate, the plan wouldn't pass the test and it would not be permitted by the government. "I'd worked with enough employees to know that the bulk of them wouldn't be willing to set aside a big chunk of pay for retirement just to save money on taxes," Benna says.

So Benna began to study paragraph k to see how he might interpret it to help his client include lower-paid workers in the retirement plan so that it would pass the test. He came up with two key concepts that made the 401(k) plan what it is today: he saw that the savings could come from regular salary rather than bonuses, and he came up with the idea of deducting contributions on a regular basis from each employee paycheck. More important, he developed the concept of employer matching funds, the key to the attractiveness of the 401(k) plans. "Neither of these was in the code," Benna says. "But I took the position that if something wasn't prohibited, you could do it."

As it turned out, his bank client didn't want to be a guinea pig and test an interpretation of the new law that hadn't been specifically laid out. So Benna's own employer, the Johnson Companies, set up the first 401(k) savings plan on January 1, 1981, as a test case. In November of that year, the Internal Revenue Service acknowledged that Benna's interpretation of paragraph k was an acceptable one.

The 401(k) plan took off almost immediately for one key reason: it allowed employers to begin shifting the immense responsibility for retirement savings to their employees. Critics see this as evil. Few of us can view the changes in corporate America over the last three decades without emotion because few of us have been untouched. But from a bird's-eye view, it was more pragmatic than evil. American companies were beginning to feel the heat of intense global competition. For many of them, it was cut costs or perish. Some of them may have done it heartlessly. But it is clear now that corporations needed to do what they could to cut costs. We live with the mixed results.

The Sky is Falling

Today, 401(k) plans hold $3 trillion in assets on behalf of 50 million active participants and millions of former employees and retirees, according to the Investment Company Institute, the mutual fund trade association (www.ici.org/401k). And the plans are, in fact, the best investment around for employees who have the opportunity to use them, even taking into account the stock market disaster in 2008.

One troubling aspect of this popularity is that corporations have spent millions of dollars to persuade employees that 401(k) plans are wonderful. But no one is being paid to look for the negatives in these plans. In the first fifteen years of their existence, all the news about 401(k) plans was good news. The financial media can sound like a thundering herd, and the herd couldn't say enough good things about 401(k) plans. Further, the soaring balances in 401(k) plans feathered a lot of nests: the employer, of course, could set up pension plans more cheaply. The spectacular growth in mutual funds can be attributed largely to the existence of 401(k) plans. Consultants, marketers, magazines and newspapers that sold advertising, perhaps even journalists, were given a shot in the arm with all the money flowing into 401(k) plans.

Lots of material written about how great these plans are and how you could get the most out of them was paid for by vendors who sold the plans. One result of this publicity was that 401(k) plans became linked to America and apple pie. They were good. They were a benefit. They would help you reverse the trend of spending your dollars and show you how to save them for retirement. Not surprisingly, then, there was little objective criticism of these plans and too little objective educational material to help employees set up and manage their plans. The cost of the plans went up and employers passed those costs on to 401(k) plan participants with no employee advocate to criticize that move.

As the plans grew, problems emerged. Some employers have insisted that the employer's contribution be in the form of company stock—or, worse yet, that the employee contribution be in the form of company stock. Some employers give participants so few options it is not possible to set up a well-diversified portfolio. Or they set up plans that cost too much. The typical 401(k) plan evolved from a low-fee product that was sponsored by the employer, to a high-fee product, as employers have shifted expenses onto their employees. Because employees pay for them, the employer no longer has an incentive to keep expenses low.

Within the past decade, as flaws have been exposed, 401(k) plans no longer enjoy their once-rosy reputations. The danger of investing in company stock was demonstrated in 2001 when Enron, the seventh-largest U.S. corporation disappeared into bankruptcy almost overnight. About 58 percent of Enron's 401(k) assets were invested in Enron stock at the end of 2000, when the stock was valued at $83 and Enron was viewed as a savvy, new-economy company. Within months, the stock traded at 45 cents a share and employees lost their jobs in the failed company as well as their 401(k) assets.

Criticisms of the plans have made investors smarter and better able to invest wisely. The plans are still a great investment. But not until you recognize that you must get educated about them and do some of the work on researching investments yourselves. Unfortunately, plan sponsors are reluctant to provide this information for fear that giving employees information on the investments will make the employers liable if employees make bad choices.

But the 401(k) plans faced their biggest test in 2008 when all sections of the market were down 40 percent, according to Benna, who now serves as a consultant for 401(k) plans, helping employers to make the plans better for employees by cutting costs, improving investment options, and working with employees to help them understand how the plans work. And that's what we intend to do here. This book will give you the information you need to understand what happened to world markets in 2008, how your 401(k) figures in it and how to best use your plan going forward.

As for Benna, his brainchild certainly didn't make him a rich man. In fact, his career mirrors that of tens of thousands of men and women in the nearly thirty years since the 401(k) plan was developed. His employer was purchased by another benefits consultant, and then another. Benna worked on a contract basis until it ran out in 1993, when he was just fifty-two. But Benna had been a partner at Johnson Companies, and he was financially able to choose what he wanted to do. He didn't want to retire. Yet he needed a flexible job schedule that would accommodate his considerable volunteer work. A deeply religious man, he sits on the boards of a seminary, a bible college, and a church, and he speaks regularly to a group of Christian businessmen.

He also wanted to do something that would increase retirement savings for rank-and-file employees rather than for the high-paid executives who hired him as an employee benefits consultant. "Most of my work up until that point had been for small-business owners and professionals," Benna says. "There was a great tendency for these people to want to get personal benefit from their companies' retirement plans and to give very little to employees."

So Benna went out on his own, setting up the 401(k) Association, whose mission he defined as "anything that would fall under protecting and promoting 401(k) plans." Benna believes 401(k) plans are politically vulnerable because they cost so much in lost tax revenues and because they don't have a special lobbying group. The members of his group, who pay a small annual fee, are mostly individual plan participants who want to keep abreast of changes in this area. But Benna also sets up 401(k) plans for very small businesses at a nominal cost—his way, he says, of giving back and helping those who really need the retirement plans. Benna's choices reflect those that most of us must make, and inasmuch as we can anticipate them and be ready, we will undoubtedly be more satisfied.

In the years since 401(k) plans were introduced, they have come to dominate the world of personal finance and financial planning advice. They have changed the path of the stock market as well as the growth of mutual funds and the financial planning profession. Dozens of articles and books urge Americans to contribute, contribute, contribute to a 401(k) plan. Every day, studies are done and articles are written to show that Americans do not save enough for retirement. When you read these studies, you should remember that they are funded by vendors like Fidelity Investments or Bank of America who have a big stake in 401(k) plans. Your contributions can become their profits.

The surveys present a black-and-white picture that is discouraging to those who are struggling along in their lives trying to figure out how to pay the mortgage and wondering whether they will survive the next round of corporate downsizings. That's been truer than ever since the devastating crash of 2008.

This book does not assume that a 401(k) plan will solve all your problems in life. Nor does it assume that saving for retirement is the only thing you have to do with your money. Instead it will try to persuade you to aim for financial independence and show you how you can use your 401(k) plan as part of your "freedom strategy." Perhaps you will not have the luxury of leaving the money in your plan until you retire. Perhaps you will not want to. But get it in there. We should be doing everything we can to increase our options. Putting money away is one of them.

In more than thirty years of writing about business and money issues—six of them as the personal finance columnist for the Sunday edition of the *New York Times*—I've learned that for most Americans, dealing with money is more about psychology and less about dollars and cents. If you are told that you need $1 million worth of life insurance, $1 million in your retirement account, and $500,000 to educate your kids, you're likely to feel discouraged, throw up your hands and give up on the whole matter of financial planning. So rather than focusing on seemingly impossible goals, it's better to buy some life insurance, put some money in a retirement account, and think a bit about college savings.

With that in mind, know that 401(k) plans can be a terrific planning tool, that they should be your first priority for saving. In this book, I'll give you some investment tips on how to get the most out of the plans. I'll also show you what you need for a comfortable retirement. But I'm not going to beat the drum for two hundred pages on why you can never expect to be anything but a wage slave. I don't believe the outlook is that grim.

I'm also going to tell you something you've probably heard before: the baby-boom generation will be working longer than their parents did. The retirement age for Social Security is already changing for that generation.

There is some good news on the "working longer" front. Studies show that baby boomers are inventing new paths for themselves. Like George Kinder, the "life planner" I mentioned earlier, many Americans are taking the time to find their passions, to search out the things they love to do best, and then doing some research to see how these passions can be shaped into a part-time avocation with growth potential. One woman quit her job of twenty-five years to indulge her passion for sailing. But she found that sailing didn't keep her mind active full-time, so she agreed to go back to her company during some of the winter months. Companies say they are responding to the desire for flex-time and are offering more options, including leaves of absence, change in workplace for summer and winter and so on.

For George Kinder, the search started as a drive to spend more time in a place that to him spoke of poetry and peace and wonder. So he opened a branch of his financial planning service in Hawaii. But, as usually happens, one thing led to another and pretty soon he saw that the type of life planning he'd done for himself could be helpful to nearly everyone and so he turned his practice to life planning and then to training life planners.

We could all learn a lesson from Kinder about the importance of taking some time and energy to pursue passion in our lives. That doesn't mean we don't have to save for retirement. But it might mean we will have a happier life and an easier and more pleasant transition into retirement as a continuation of that life. The American Association of Retired Persons (AARP) published a study in May 2009 that showed that older workers and retirees moving into different lines of work reported greater job satisfaction, chiefly because of less stress and more flexible work schedules.[2]

I hope this book will set you thinking about how you might do that. I have put together a collection of short essays on the tasks you need to do to get the most from your 401(k) plan. They cover everything from getting into the plan to getting out of it and maximizing your money in retirement. Although they move in a somewhat logical order, the book is designed so that each "essay/thought" is presented on a single two-page spread. That means you can open the book anywhere and get one little piece of advice or information. You needn't read the book from front to back. You can dip in and read something you find interesting, or something you need to know right now. This will not be the end of the work you need to do. Lifetime planning is a big job and a critical one. Putting money away into a 401(k) plan is an important starting point.

2. Richard W. Johnson, Janette Kawachi, and Eric K. Lewis, "Older Workers on the Move: Recareering in Later Life," The Urban Institute, May 2009, http://www.aarp.org/research/work/employment/2009_08_recareering.html.

PART ONE

THE NEW RETIREMENT LANDSCAPE

What Happened?

Many investors, including those in 401(k) plans, feel frustrated, angry, and let down by the near-collapse of the U.S. financial structure. "Near" might be too generous. It seems the only way Wall Street could be shored up was to spend our tax money to put the finger in the dike of rampant greed and irresponsibility. Investors—as well as all other taxpayers—have a right to be outraged about it. But we must also accept the fact that if the government allowed the banking system to give way, we would need to go back to barter and trade. So it's not a question of whether it's right to hold up this rickety system that other people have all but destroyed; we can't move ahead, any of us, until we have a sound banking system.

I've been writing about money long enough to remember the magazine covers of the 1980s—young couples planning to retire at fifty and live the good life. In the 1980s, retirement seemed to be the definition of the good life.

Why? The eighties were a time of conspicuous consumption, almost to decadence. Baby boomers who had belatedly entered the job market felt they needed to catch up, to make a lot of money, to have two children, and, because they were older now, and richer, to create a magazine-cover family.

So the Boomers began getting pregnant, and never had anyone been pregnant like this before! They must read books to babies in the womb. They must play classical music for the fetus. They must have hand-made European chocolates and Ben and Jerry's ice cream to satisfy cravings. And the babies! Never had there been babies like this before. They needed handcrafted European cribs and handmade quilts from offshore islands and personalized silver tippie cups. The needs of these late blooming boomers and their kids made many companies like the Swedish clothing designer Hannah Andersen rich.

Status was best achieved by finding new sources for expensive baby clothing and toys and by being ahead of the curve—but not too far, in case no one followed you.

I wrote a column for *Working Woman* magazine in the eighties, and we decided to do a series of money stories—a financial makeover of sorts like the ones made famous by *Money* magazine—that would appeal to the working women of that decade. We found just the right format: A twelve-month makeover for a Yuppie couple, written like a screenplay, to show that our couple recognized the top-of-the-line baby buggies and infant shoes and the rest but they decided to cut corners—at Starbucks® for example—so they could buy a proper weekend cottage in a place that the insiders would know was trendy. I guess our message was that putting together a financial plan was necessary but only if it preserved the "must-haves" to show colleagues that this couple was in the know. Spending money on babies, on family, more money than anyone else, replaced the need to retire at fifty. When you turned fifty, your child would only be five years old. What about graduate school? Medical school? Juilliard? Goals changed.

Still, professional couples in the eighties were on the fast track. Working women needed tips on how to get promoted and have a baby at the same time. They were willing to work one hundred hours a week if necessary to buy those French clothes and Italian suits and handbags. Perhaps it was that people worked too many hours a week and hated their jobs and couldn't wait to be free of them, so they believed that if they worked even harder, they could leave their jobs sooner to have fun. Most people came to see that this was a delusion. If it wasn't a delusion before, it certainly became one in 1987 when the stock market crashed.

We've learned a lot about retirement over the past twenty years. Most of us no longer expect to retire at forty-five or fifty. We don't see our lives broken into two pieces: work and retirement. Boomers are growing older. Now they can't retire, or don't want to. Americans in the twenty-first century want to integrate their work with their passion. They want to have a good life now and later. Many of them are finding ways to do that—such as developing a hobby into an avocation and then turning it into a business. Or going back to school and changing directions.

A friend of mine, an expert in early American artifacts, worked as a museum consultant. She quit to study Thai massage, moved to Thailand to learn more, married a Thai Buddhist monk, and came back to New York to set up her practice with husband and baby son in tow. How many people do you know who are dumping traditional careers for a more holistic approach to work and taking up practices such as healing arts or alternative medicine or a spiritual pursuit? The modern investor wants to have a job that satisfies more than just a financial constraint.

When I compare the tone of magazines I wrote for in the eighties with those today, I see big changes. Fewer people want to learn about how to get the promotion, how to get ahead of coworkers. More want to learn about finding zest in life. The focus has changed from how much money can I make to how can I find peace and fulfillment? I expect that trend to accelerate as Americans begin to reassess what happened in the credit crisis of 2008. People today are coming to realize that if you don't feel excited about life now, retirement will change nothing.

One of the truths that came out of this culture change is that many of us learned that we need lifetime goals. We've all heard the stories about Americans who work hard for forty years and then, when they quit, they realize that working hard for forty years was the only goal they'd set in life. They've reached the goal and now they drift off, not into a blissful retirement, but into a place where they've lost their definition, where the edges are blurring, where they have no more goals, no more passion.

Americans are living much longer. If you live to one hundred, you can't spend half your life in retirement. Few people can afford fifty years of retirement spending.

The new retirement landscape looks much different. Still, I do know one executive who retired early and created a beautiful life after full-time work. But it happened a while ago. Stan Breitbard retired as national director of personal finance at Price Waterhouse in 1995 at the age of fifty-six. He wanted a change and fully expected to find another full-time position somewhere near his home in Los Angeles. It didn't work out that way, though.

Stan does have many passions: James Joyce, improving financial literacy, travel, education, knowledge, and his wife, Ronda. He can sound like a one-man band beating against the evils of financial ignorance and how it ruins the lives of so many Americans. Just because you are an accountant or a businessman or a lawyer doesn't mean you know how to manage your personal finances, Stan says.

One of the first things he did after retirement was to develop a program for teaching personal finance to students who were working on their master's degrees in business administration. Stan says he was astounded that most students didn't understand that a financial plan encompassed dreams and passions, that it included everything you want to accomplish in life along with a strategy to use your resources— human and financial—to achieve it. He taught personal finance to MBAs at Berkeley for seven years and "loved it," he says. But then it was time to move on again.

In 1998, he co-founded the California Jump$tart Coalition (www.cajumpstart.org). California Jump$tart focuses on personal finance education for children and teenagers in school. I spoke at one of his meetings in Sacramento and was surprised to see hundreds of people there, all enthusiastic about boosting the financial literacy of children and teens.

Stan also formed a Los Angeles James Joyce Reading Group and acts as facilitator. That group celebrated its tenth anniversary in 2008. He presented a paper on *Ulysses* at the International James Joyce Conference in 2007. He is treasurer of his condo homeowner association, a community of three hundred units, and he and Ronda welcomed four grandchildren between 2004 and 2008. Now that's a retirement! "Of course," Stan says, "I rethink what I'm doing constantly. I think about where I want to live, what I want to do, how I want to work." This is the portion of Stan's life that is called "retirement" and one most would be happy to emulate.

My point is your working life and your retirement life are not two distinct phases, one drudgery and one pleasure. Those who work successfully and retire successfully knit the two together, almost seamlessly. But it is not as easy as it looks. It requires a great deal of thought about who you are, what you want, what you enjoy, and where you're going. And a great deal of planning. In a sense, this is the toughest part of financial planning because it requires facing up to who you are and what you dream about. Top financial planners, like Stan Breitbard, say they have lost clients because they've asked them to face these questions when all the clients want to talk about is which stocks to buy.

Stan asked his MBA students at Berkeley to draw up a five-year financial plan for themselves. The students fell into three groups. The first concentrated on simple bookkeeping tasks: Paying off bills, developing a filing system, getting organized. The second group focused on saving and investing and included some long-term goals. But only the third group looked at real financial planning—dreaming dreams and thinking about where they would go in life and how they would get there.

You wouldn't be reading a book about 401(k) plans if you weren't thinking about your retirement or perhaps worrying about it. So much of what we read is designed to make us frightened that we won't have enough money to retire. When you think of retirement, I urge you to think of it in the broadest possible terms. Don't think of it as a compromise. Spin out all your dreams. Stretch to include everything in life that you might want to be and do. Now you're ready to start planning.

Not Your Father's Gold Watch

WHEREVER YOU ARE in your working life—first job out of college or at the top of your game —take a few minutes to think about what you can expect from a job or career and what you might expect later, when it's over.

Just out of college? You shouldn't have a career set in stone. Few people end up doing exactly what they prepared to do in college. Some who do end up feeling stultified later because they feel they've never had the time or place to grow and explore.

Recent college graduates face a particularly difficult job market. Don't despair. Look for a job in an area that mirrors your talents and interests, even if it is low-level. But do look forward and dream. Don't get caught in the financial needs of the moment, focusing on paying off college loans, saving money for a great vacation or the perfect honeymoon or a down payment on a house so that you spend money as fast as you earn it and never have the luxury to reflect on what you might have done. Life is what happens when you're busy paying the bills and struggling to keep your head above water.

Failing to look into the future is one of the biggest mistakes working Americans make. We're constantly reminded that we're never saving enough for retirement. That's an old tune. What about that stretch of time between now and retirement? If we're saving everything for retirement, we're probably not stretching our lives to become the most we can be now, and later.

Work life in America was redefined in the 1980s and 1990s as more than 43 million jobs disappeared. Many new jobs appeared. But too many that were lost belonged to higher-paid, white-collar workers—those employees who looked forward to a pension and a comfortable retirement.

Middle managers were replaced by contract workers. "Consultant" is the euphemism for many of those who today earn low wages and receive no benefits. Americans who were forced into "early retirement" in their fifties often found they had to return to work in their seventies as grocery clerks or inventory stockers.

This revolutionary change in the workplace will be followed by a revolutionary change in retirement. Don't get depressed. Do think about what you will do with your work life and your non-work life and how you might merge them together in a way that is satisfying.

Charles Handy, a professor and author on organizational change, made some suggestions in his book, *The Age of Unreason* (Harvard Business School Press, 1998). When Handy wrote in 1990 that working at a corporation was no longer a viable career path for most people, it seemed startling. Two decades later, it seems obvious.

Handy, who began his career as an oil executive and then became a teacher and writer, predicted that workers in the twenty-first century would fit into one of three types: managers and technicians who will run the corporations, unskilled clerks and laborers, and those who work on a contract basis. Not only will many of us spend our working lives as self-employed contractors, Handy wrote, but all of us will work until a much later age. Even those managers and technicians who work as employees will remain in their jobs only until age fifty-five or so, he predicted, at which point they will have fifteen or twenty more work years.

This future is now. To prepare, Handy recommends that you develop a portfolio of skills, services, and products that you can sell to corporations and to others in the marketplace. When his own two children left college, he told them: "I hope you won't look for a job in a corporation." Instead, he advised them: "Look for customers. If you have a saleable skill, you can always work."

Of course demographics play a role too. As Americans live longer and enjoy better health, most of us will want to be busy and productive. Whether you are just starting out in your career, you are at midpoint, or you are nearing the finish line, work on the skills you need and develop the talents you have. Retirement at sixty or sixty-five will no longer be an option for most people working today. Those who have a portfolio of skills will be able to pick and choose what they will do and when they want to do it. For them, a blend of work and leisure can be a pleasure. It will solve the "problems" of both work and retirement.

"Management" Is Not a Career Choice

WHAT IS YOUR PASSION? What do you do well? Of course we'll always have managers. But you need to develop a skill that you can perform on your own. Here is the problem for millions of middle managers who were "downsized" or "outplaced" or just plain fired as the American economy grew leaner and maybe meaner. As corporations became flatter and team management replaced the management hierarchy, few people are being paid simply to manage other people. If you want to succeed, you must identify something you can do that commands a fee or a salary. Managing is not it.

It's not easy for many people to discover what their skills and talents are beyond the title a corporation gives them. "But we all have a lot of neglected talents," says Handy. "It's a matter of redefining yourself. You need help because you've only seen yourself in one light."

To free up your thinking about what you're good at, what you enjoy doing, and how you might turn that into a career, Handy suggests that you go to twenty people you know and ask each to tell you one thing you do very well. Handy instructed a forty-eight-year-old advertising executive who had just lost his job to do that exercise. "It was sort of embarrassing," this former adman told Handy. "I got twenty answers and not one of them was advertising." Instead, this man was told that he was very creative, good at organizing teams, presenting ideas, leading people, selecting wines, and recalling historical details. What could be done with those skills?

This one-time adman set up a business taking people on tours of battlefields and other historical sights and vineyards throughout Europe. "He was able to redefine his whole life," Handy says. "It was a nice example of what you can do with some original thinking." It's also an example of the rewards for stretching far afield when you think about what you do well. Many of us have landed in jobs or careers by happenstance or as a result of a pull in youth to "become someone." Many stuck to their jobs long after they stopped feeling any satisfaction from them. We should always be alive and alert to a new opportunity that might have our name on it.

Consider what outplacement firms do for those who are laid off. You might be asked to write an autobiography, breaking up your life into chapters: early childhood, grade school, high school, college, first job. When you get to career, think broadly of the tasks you have done rather than what you've been called such as "administrative assistant," or "human resources director." We tend to think of our career as our recent job.

But even if you have spent your career at one company, you have no doubt had several separate and distinct jobs. Think of a particular task you have enjoyed and duties you've performed well—on the job, in school, or in volunteer projects. A young woman I know who worked as an administrator in a corporation and looked forward all day to yoga class, took a job with a yoga foundation, and a pay cut. Now she travels around the world teaching yoga as well as serving as administrator of the yoga foundation.

When people go through this process, they often discover that there was one particular stop in their career where they loved what they were doing. As they moved along, that passion somehow got lost or misplaced as they became subsumed by corporate politics and management duties. We believe that the path to success must lead up to the next rung of the ladder even if we don't perform well at that level and don't enjoy the work.

For me, it was the promotion to editor or manager that always sent me looking for a writing job at another newspaper. I didn't want to manage other people and tell them how to write. I wanted to write. Thinking through this process helps many people discover what it was they really liked to do. Perhaps that's why so many people who go through the painful layoff process say later: "It's the best thing that ever happened to me."

Even if you are happy in your job now, hone your skills. Whatever you do, you will need computer skills. You need to know how to use the computer and how to find your way around the Internet. Develop your skills in writing, communications, foreign languages, and mathematics. Every year, aim to take on a new area of study. For me, it's been theology recently. I don't expect to become a priest or a Biblical scholar. But I find it fascinating and I'm willing to take the risk that it will pave a new road for me at some point. Already it enriches my life. Maybe you'd like to study music or poetry or art or physics or international relations. Everything you learn makes you a more fascinating person and more attractive to potential employers or clients.

Dip a Toe In

CHANCES ARE GOOD that at some time in your career, you will work for yourself. Many people dream of owning their own business. Many others are terrified at the prospect. Not all parents suggest that their children develop skills and learn to market them, as Handy does. Many still believe that security comes from a good career at a big company with great benefits. I remember when people thought that IBM was untouchable, would always be on top, and would never reduce benefits. That was before the rounds of layoffs beginning in the 1990s, the elimination of the defined benefit plan, and the streamlining of benefits.

Now many employees view companies like IBM—and those that laid off hundreds of workers after the 2008 market crash—as villains. In most cases, that's simply not true. In a global economy, and especially a struggling global economy, corporations simply cannot take care of employees for life. Rather than viewing this as a betrayal, we'd be better off accepting it as reality and putting our energy into moving ahead. Playing the victim only makes it harder to take charge and find your own solution.

Depending indefinitely on a paycheck from a corporation is a foolhardy approach to the future. Wherever you are in your work life, you need an escape plan. You need a skill for which someone will pay you. The best way to discover one is to think about how you might set up an independent business. There is almost no job that can't be done on a contract basis. All kinds of people thrive as entrepreneurs. You need a passion for what you do, discipline, and hard work.

Many talented, entrepreneurial people move in and out of corporations. They develop their skills working for one or more employers and then set up their own shop—as designers, writers, carpenters, electricians, software developers, or accountants—and begin to acquire clients. Sometimes they discover that one client is consuming more and more time and providing more challenging work. They might join that company as an employee.

But these employees don't resemble those of the 1960s. Modern workers have a portable skill set. They never become lulled into thinking the corporation will take care of them when they get sick, when they get old, when the company is acquired, or when new management takes over. Nor do they become rigid with fear when these things happen. Successful workers in the twenty-first century will focus on their own skills and on how to develop them rather than on corporate politics and how to stay on the right side of the boss. You should always be on the lookout for ways to develop your own skills. Look for opportunities to take on new projects, to speak, to make presentations, or to appear on radio or television. Don't back away from difficult assignments. They will help you grow.

Here are some other things to consider:

■ **Risk.** Don't brush off the possibility of self-employment just because it scares you to death. Every successful entrepreneur feels exactly the same way. One of the biggest risks people take is putting all their eggs in one basket by relying on the same employer for salary, benefits, pension, and then investing in the company stock.

■ **Marketing.** Many people with terrific skills simply don't know how to let people know that they're available. This task is much simpler than it used to be. In the small town where I live, most people prefer to rely on independent computer consultants, plumbers, roofers, florists, acupuncturists, and nearly every other service they need. In every case, if you are good at what you do and start doing it, the word will get out.

■ **Fees.** You must be able to figure out how much to charge and stick to your guns. Remember that you will be paying your own benefits. If you use an hourly fee, you should take into account the years you spent building expertise in your field when you set the fee.

■ **Professional growth.** You still need mentors. But they will not be the obvious ones from your workplace. Constantly weigh the relative merits of pumping out more work or, say, attending seminars to learn more about your specialty. Create a balance, too, between projects that pay well but offer little challenge and those that pay less but offer growth opportunity.

Calculate Retirement Needs

"BORING," I HEAR you saying. Yes. And sobering, too. Some Americans worry about retirement practically from the time they start their careers. When I wrote for a magazine called *Working Woman* in the 1980s, women worried about it a lot. The magazine learned from a survey that even women with considerable wealth saw themselves living in a sinkhole and eating cat food when they were in their seventies. *Working Woman* called it the Bag Lady Syndrome. Since then, it's become a term that most Americans recognize as an unrealistic fear that many women have about their later years.

I'm not intending to discriminate against men here, because I'm sure that men can fret just as well as women. But in the 1980s, the bull market created a good deal of optimism. In the autumn of 2009, many investors again felt optimistic after watching the stock market, as measured by the Standard & Poor's Index of 500 Stocks rise 60 percent off its March lows. Yet this time is different because those lows were so low and virtually no one's retirement account escaped the plunge.

I don't believe we should beat ourselves up because we haven't saved as much as other thirty-year-olds or fifty-year-olds or retirees. Still, it's time to focus on the numbers.

There are lots of charts, tables and software programs to help you find out how much money you will need for retirement. Most assume that you will need about 75 to 80 percent of your working income to maintain a comfortable lifestyle in retirement. Chances are your 401(k) plan provider has a software program that you can use to keep track of your portfolio and also to make projections about how much you will need at retirement and how much you will have. Take advantage of that.

TABLE 1.1 is a simple but useful chart prepared by Steven E. Norwitz, chief of corporate communications at T. Rowe Price & Associates, the Baltimore-based mutual fund company. Norwitz had planned to retire in 2009, but he's back at work at least half time. His chart helps you figure out how much of your annual income you need to save going forward depending on how old you are and how much you have already saved.

The three boxes ask for the amount you've already saved for retirement, divided by your annual salary. To make it simple, suppose you've saved $50,000, you are 45 years old, and you earn $100,000 a year. If you divide your $50,000 savings by your $100,000 salary, you will get .5. That means you've saved half of your current salary. Read across the top of the chart to see the 0 times, .5 times, 1 times, etc. Your savings fall in the .5x column. Because you are 45 years old, this chart suggests that you must save 33 percent of your salary from now on, assuming you want to have enough money for retirement at age 65.

The chart assumes your salary increases 3 percent a year and that you earn 8 percent on your investments in a tax-deferred account before retirement.

Table 1.1   Percentage You'll Need to Save for Retirement

Example: *If you are 35 years old and have already saved half of your salary (multiple =.5), you need to save at least 15% of your salary each year from now until your retirement date*

Amount you have already saved for retirement· ÷ Annual salary· = Multiple: Round this number to the nearest multiple below

Multiple of amount of salary already saved

Current age	0x	.5x	1x	1.5x	2x	2.5x	3x	
25	10%	8%	5%	3%	–	–	–	If you're in this range, your savings strategy is on track
30	14%	11%	8%	5%	2%	–	–	
35	18%	15%	12%	9%	6%	3%	–	
40	25%	22%	19%	15%	12%	9%	5%	
45	37%	33%	29%	25%	21%	18%	14%	
50	56%	51%	47%	42%	38%	33%	29%	
55	95%	89%	83%	77%	71%	65%	59%	

Note: *These results are based on your age and how much you have already saved, assuming you retire at age 65. The chart assumes your salary increases 3% annually for inflation and that you earn 8% on your investments in a tax deferred account before retirement when you retire, it assumes your initial withdrawal amount will be 4% of your balance at that time.*

Source: T. Rowe Price.

How to Fill the Gaps

CALCULATING RETIREMENT needs may not be fun. But figuring out what changes you can make might be interesting, particularly if they are nearly effortless. A good retirement software program can help you look at all your assets—retirement accounts like 401(k) plans, pension plans, Individual Retirement Accounts (IRAs), as well as the equity in your home, the cash value in your life insurance, and other savings and assets you might have—and translate them into retirement income.

You can plug in your salary and your current rate of savings and see how much you fall short. Then you can see what happens if you save a little more or if you invest more aggressively. If you are in your twenties, the result of even a tiny change can be startling. Wherever you are, changing your habits just a bit can make a big difference.

The best place to begin is your company's human resources department. Most employers want their employees to grasp the enormity of the need to save for retirement. And they're doing what they can to help. Many provide tools that are customized to use your company's 401(k) plan and pension to help you see what you can expect from them and where you might fall short. Employers want their employees to save, and they want them to understand what their savings will mean when projected out thirty or forty years. Remember though that these numbers are not a guarantee. Every calculator does some things right and makes some assumptions that might turn out to be inaccurate. Employer sponsors also differ widely in the amount of help and information they provide.

On one extreme is a company like IBM, a traditional leader in the employee benefits arena. When IBM makes a change in its benefits plans, it takes great effort to make certain employees understand the new rules and can make the best possible use of them. When I wrote a personal finance column for the *New York Times*, I made a couple of visits to IBM's head quarters in Armonk, NY, to get a demonstration of a new software program IBM was distributing to all employees. IBM's purpose was twofold: to help them chart a course to retirement by manipulating budget assumptions and pension options and also to make certain they didn't stay around too long. At the time, IBM had built an enviable reputation for avoiding layoffs. And the company still hoped to avoid them. (As we all know, that didn't work out.)

IBM's software package showed employees what they could expect in inflation-adjusted dollars from each portion of the company's retirement plan as well as from Social Security. It also helped them determine how they could change the picture by saving, say, 1 percent more of salary or taking a little bit more investment risk to try to produce an additional 1 percentage point in return. The software showed how much of a gap an employee faced between expected income and what might be needed at retirement. And it suggested ways to close the gap, such as contributing more to a 401(k) plan. The IBM story is an interesting one because it illustrates how what was once the mightiest of companies was forced to trim benefits to stay in the game—and how it tried to help employees as it did so. Since then, many employers and consultants have done similar things. And third-party advisors have developed programs that take an objective look at different types of plans.

In June 1999 for example, Nobel Laureate Bill Sharpe introduced an online software product called Financial Engines to help 401(k) sponsors better understand the plans and to help participants make better investment choices. Sharpe offered the same analytical tools he uses with his pension-fund clients to participants in 401(k) plans. Financial Engines (www.financialengines.com) has grown rapidly over the last decade and now works with many companies that sponsor 401(k) plans—such as IBM—and also with those that offer 401(k) plans, such as Fidelity, Vanguard, and T. Rowe Price. Most employers sponsor some type of analytical tool for employees to work with retirement needs. Check with your employer to see what it is.

It *is* sobering to see just how much money it will cost to support yourself without any employment income coming in. Don't get discouraged about it. Save as much as you can. Learn about investing. And think about how you will supplement this nest egg.

Will You Get a Pension?

SOME OF TODAY'S retirees—at least a few—enjoy rich pension benefits from corporate plans, many of which were set up after World War II to attract workers and to retain them in a booming economy. These plans are called defined benefit plans because they define the annual pension benefit you receive. The employer foots the bill for the entire plan, putting the money aside, investing it, and taking the responsibility for making certain it is available to pay out benefits.

Defined benefit plans were designed to reward loyal employees who spent their entire careers with one company. The benefit is heavily weighted toward the later working years, when the employee's salary is highest. A good plan should replace about 50 percent of income for an employee with thirty years of service.

But few Americans at mid-career today have spent their working lives with a single employer. Instead, young workers typically change jobs frequently to gain broad experience. Many forty-five-year-olds are not vested in any pension plan at all.

The benefit from a traditional pension is calculated as a percent of your final salary times years of service with the company. A typical defined benefit plan might provide 1.2 percent to 1.5 percent of the average of your final three years of compensation times your years of service as an annual pension. Suppose your average salary over your last three years of work is $100,000 a year. In that case, 1.5 percent is $1,500. If you have been with the company for forty years, your annual pension would be $60,000. Work twenty-five years, and you earn $37,500; five years earns you $7,500. But each of these calculations assume you spent your final working years, when your salary is highest, with the employer that sponsors a defined benefit plan. If, instead, you spend your first five years with this employer, your benefit will be peanuts.

So job hopping reduces the benefit substantially. When you leave an employer at age forty, your pension benefit at age sixty-five will be calculated based on the salary you earned twenty-five years earlier, with no adjustment for inflation. One executive I know spent eighteen years of his work life with a large industrial company with an excellent pension plan, leaving when he was forty-seven. When he retired at sixty-five, his pension from this previous employer was not enough to cover his utility bill each month. That's the way employers want to set up defined benefit plans: To reward the career worker for his loyalty.

To illustrate the penalty for job hoppers, retirement actuary Ethan E. Kra calculated benefits for three employees, each with forty years of employment, the same final salary, and the same pension benefit formula. The first, who spent all forty years with the same employer, receives 60 percent of his final salary as a pension benefit. The second, who worked at two employers for twenty years each, receives 39 percent of final salary. The third, who worked at four employers for ten years each, receives just 31 percent.

It's common to say that employers have let their employees down by reducing defined benefit pensions. I think that's a cop-out. Many employees of the twenty-first century do not relish a career with a single employer. They want, instead, to create a career path of their choice by working for various employers and including stints of self employment. Obviously, many more important things shape career decisions than what type of pension you receive. Still, understanding how benefits in these plans are affected by salary and years of service remains important.

By working longer, you increase the time during which you will have a regular income, and you increase your assets and eventual pension at the same time you decrease the years spent consuming those assets. Federal law mandates that your employer continue to credit years of service for pension purposes if you work beyond normal retirement age. If you receive salary increases, you will also be increasing your pay for purposes of calculating your pension. The eventual pension increase reflects what is called an "actuarial equivalent," meaning you should get the same amount of money over your expected lifespan no matter when you decide to retire.

Will You Get Anything from Social Security?

THE SOCIAL SECURITY SYSTEM is in deep trouble. Good financial advisors are telling clients to start viewing Social Security as a subsidy for lower-income individuals rather than a benefit that we will all collect. One planner tells me: "You may get something, but you probably won't get it until age seventy, and it won't be worth what you think it will be worth."

Social Security income has never been adequate to provide for a comfortable retirement. But for many of today's retirees, it provides a reasonable base. Even that is changing. And it will change rapidly as the baby boomers begin to retire this year. If the system were to continue as it is today, it is expected to start paying out more each year in benefits than it collects in taxes after 2012. Sure there are economists and other "experts" who still argue that Social Security is just bent a little bit and that it will right itself. That isn't going to happen. So don't you be in the group counting on this bubble to keep growing.

Changing demographics are straining the system. When the first Social Security checks were mailed out in 1937, more than forty workers were paying withholding taxes to support each retiree. Today just three workers support each retiree. And that will drop to two workers per retiree by the year 2030.

Americans are living much longer, too. When the system was set up in the 1930s, few people lived long enough to collect Social Security. In contrast, retirees today may have twenty to thirty years or more ahead of them. As a result retirees collect much more than they paid into the system, putting a bigger burden on working people.

Bandages have been applied to the system. For instance, normal retirement age will increase gradually to age sixty-seven—and then perhaps beyond. Higher-income retirees pay tax on benefits, another trend that is certain to accelerate. This remains clear: middle and upper income taxpayers will get a haircut on their Social Security benefits before we get much further into the twenty-first century.

Still, the government's largest and most popular program is unlikely to disappear. Neither political party wants to take the blame for cutting benefits and/or increasing taxes. The Bush Administration pushed a plan to privatize the system. After the 2008–2009 market crash, critics of the Bush plan pointed out that things would have been even worse had the system been privatized. The benefit forecast has grown even more grim since then. After six months in office, the Obama Administration has not yet proposed a plan.

Possible solutions over the past ten years have included investing in the stock market (all the money is now invested in government bonds) as well as cutting benefits and hiking taxes. But that was before the market crashes of 2000 and 2008. Even though investors seem to be going back into the market in the fourth quarter of 2009, I doubt that policy makers will have the courage to put more money at risk.

Will "experts" feel the same way about "privatizing" Social Security now? About investing some of the money in the stock market? How will the rest of us feel? The years 2000 to 2003 and more especially 2008 to 2009 have changed our thinking (we hope) about financial and economic and employment questions. Few of us feel secure in our investments in our homes, in our jobs, or in the stock market. Nor do we feel certain about the future of Social Security. The only certain thing is that Social Security needs to be reformed. In the meantime, keep track of your earnings and benefits.

Check Earnings and Benefits

DON'T DESPAIR OVER Social Security; don't get bogged down in anxiety about retirement benefits, earnings, savings, or other short-falls. Use your energy to keep moving ahead. You will get something from Social Security, but it's not clear what it will be. Social Security is unlikely to disappear. But the crystal ball is cloudy on how benefits might change.

Smart financial planning requires that you stay on course and read all the road signs. Many people believed they were on target for a comfortable retirement until the global markets collapsed in the fall of 2008 and investors lost 30 percent, 40 percent, 50 percent, and more of their savings. Some investors who gave their money to Bernard Madoff and his Ponzi scheme lost everything. But anxiety will not help. Try to stay on course and be flexible.

Even if Social Security benefits do shrink before you retire—or especially if they shrink—you want to be certain that you get what you've earned from the system. To do that, check on your recorded earnings and expected benefits. The Social Security Administration mails annual statements to workers and former workers age twenty-five and over.

Social Security benefits are based on your lifetime earnings. If your earnings get reported inaccurately to Social Security or if the Social Security Administration records them inaccurately, it could affect your benefits. The Social Security Administration is not required to correct any error in an earnings statement that is more than three years old. When I checked my own benefits the first time, I discovered I hadn't received credit for three years of earnings because I don't use my husband's surname and our income tax records had become jumbled at the Social Security Administration. Those years, which happened to be my highest earning years, were reported nowhere.

The burden is on you to make certain your records are accurate and up to date. When you get married or divorced or report your earnings on a joint return when you did not do so before, it's time to check your earnings record.

That's pretty easy to do. Call Social Security at 800-772-1213 and follow the automated instructions to request a copy of your Social Security earnings and benefits estimates. You may also go to www.ssa.gov to check earnings and benefits and to find answers to other questions about Social Security such as when is the best time to apply for benefits. You might be suspicious that you'll get an answer that favors the system rather than your pocketbook. But that's not necessarily true. Benefit start dates as well as tax implications and the effect on future benefits have become a complex area. Be sure you know all the rules.

In addition to the annual statements, Social Security will respond to any worker who requests a statement at any time. The statement shows your estimated benefits if you stop working at age sixty-two, at your full retirement age, which will be at sixty-six or sixty-seven, and at age seventy, when you would earn additional benefits for working longer.

It also shows estimated disability benefits for you and your spouse and children. But the statement warns that the law governing benefit amounts may well change because by 2041, payroll taxes collected will not be enough to pay scheduled benefits.

The statements issued at the end of 2008 noted that "the Social Security system is facing serious financial problems, and action is needed soon to make sure the system will be sound when today's younger workers are ready for retirement."

Take the time to read the statement and check your earnings record to make certain it reflects your work history. If you are nearing retirement age, take a look at the web site as well where you will find help in calculating benefits. If there is a mistake in your record, request a correction immediately.

The Rule of 72

INVESTORS ARE ALWAYS looking for that one magic investment that will make their fortune. The closest thing you will get to magic in investing is the compounding of interest. What that means is that your earnings generate their own earnings so that, seemingly by magic, money begets more money and the money you invested doubles, triples, and quadruples. Albert Einstein is alleged to have called the compounding of interest the greatest mathematical discovery of all time.

When an inexperienced investor thinks about saving for a goal, he typically estimates how much he needs and divides it by the number of years—or months—that he has to meet his goal. So to save $10,000 in five years, he might figure he needed to stash away $2,000 a year. He's wrong.

Time is the magic ingredient here. The power of compounding means that even a tiny sum of money can grow into a colossus given enough time. Consider the $24 paid by the Dutch for the island of Manhattan in 1626. Had it been invested at 7 percent, it would have grown to 4.03 trillion by the end of 2008, assuming of course that it wasn't invested in the stock market in 2008.

Few of us have three or four centuries to wait for our money to grow. But some of us *are* young. And for the young, time is a beautiful asset. Let's assume a twenty-one-year-old wants to accumulate $1 million to retire at age sixty-five. Assuming that the money returns an average of 8 percent a year, this young worker would need to put away just $2587.25 each year. (This example assumes the investor is using a tax-deferred account, such as a 401(k) account.)

Of course, some of us are *not* young. But time and the rate of return make an enormous difference for every investor. Even if you are already sixty-five, you might have twenty to thirty years ahead of you—plenty of time to take advantage of the power of compounding.

Thus, investment return is a function of both time and return. To see how the interplay between these two works, investors use a handy rule of thumb called "The Rule of 72." If you pick an annual rate of return and divide it into 72, the answer will show you how long it will take to double your money if you achieve that return.

Try it. If you earn 3 percent on a bank savings account, your money will double in twenty-four years. But if you are an active and aggressive investor who can figure out a way to earn a return of 20 percent, your money will double over 3.6 years. (Very few investors can accomplish this over time.) If you earn 10 percent, your money would double in 7.2 years. You can also turn the rule on its head to show you what interest rate you must earn in order to double your money to meet a specific goal. Say you have $10,000 and you want to double that in five years to buy a house. What interest rate must you earn? Divide 72 by 5 and you will see that you would need to earn 14.4 per cent a year for the next five years.

In the investing environment during the first decade of the twenty-first century, that interest rate is virtually unattainable. If you could achieve it, you would need to take on so much risk that you could be in danger of losing everything.

As you set up your 401(k) plan and select your investments, keep in mind the power of time and the magic of compounding. Even a small amount of money that earns a low return can grow into a mountain. But if you invest a substantial amount of money and earn a good return, it can help you achieve independence.

Although it is not implicit in compounding of interest, this principle works best with money left untouched. Trading, buying, selling, and fussing with your money all diminish the return.

10

Start Early

IF YOU'RE TWENTY-FIVE years old, saving probably sounds like punishment. Maybe you've just finished four to six years of college and money was tight. And now you're ready to spend. In many cases, particularly in a recessionary economy, there's not enough money from that first job to stretch to buy all the things you need. I know a savings account was nowhere on my priority list when I finished school.

But consider this: You may not have lots of money. But you have something far more valuable: Time. Time can turn a grain of sand into a mountain or $1,000 into a million bucks, thanks to the power of compound interest. Compounding means your money can earn money. (See p. 44 on the Rule of 72.) If a twenty-five-year-old puts $10,000 in an investment that earns 8 percent a year and leaves it for forty years, she will have more than $217,245, thanks to the magic of compounding. Of course, few twenty-five-year-olds have $10,000 to spare. But putting money away regularly is the best way to put yourself on the road to riches—or independence.

Parents and teachers have tried to teach this simple lesson to children and students for countless years. Most young adults have ignored the lesson and, instead of saving, run up big debts to buy all those things they've wanted, but couldn't afford when they were living with their parents or going to college. For my part, I didn't run up debt, but I did spend the money—nearly every dollar of it.

Think of it this way: The decisions you make about money have little to do with economics, dollars and cents, how much you have, or how much you earn. Instead, they have to do with psychology: with how you feel about yourself and with your habits. If you feel good about yourself, you don't need to spend lavishly to prove you're worth it.

Or at least that's what the research of Tahira K. Hira, a professor of personal finance and consumer behavior at Iowa State University in Ames, says. Hira spent several years studying personal bankruptcies in Scotland, Japan, and the United States, looking for patterns among those who ran into financial difficulties. She found them: low self-esteem, difficult family relationships, unhappy experiences at school. But she also found that many people with money problems could address them by facing up to them. What better time to do that then when your just getting going and have years to practise good money habits?

If you can establish a habit of regular saving when you are just starting out in your career, it will be one of the most important things you ever do for yourself. Make it small to start. Just $10 a week if you like. But make the decision to get started. And discipline yourself to do it regularly.

Start Early

Suppose you put $1,000 a year in a tax-deferred savings account. The chart shows how much you will have depending on when you begin—from age 25 through age 60—and how much you will earn.

		2% Return	4% Return	6% Return	8% Return
Starting Age	25	$60,401.98	$95,025.52	$154,761.97	$259,056.52
	30	$49,994.48	$73,652.22	$111,434.78	$172,316.80
	35	$40,568.08	$56,084.94	$79,058.19	$113,283.21
	40	$32,030.30	$41,645.91	$54,864.51	$73,105.94
	45	$24.297.31	$29,778.08	$36,785.59	$45,761.96
	50	$17,293.42	$20,023.59	$23,275.97	$27,152.10
	55	$10,949.72	$12,006.11	$13,180.79	$14,486.56
	60	$5,204.00	$5,416.32	$5,637.09	$5,866.60

Why Choose the 401(k) Plan?

NO MATTER WHAT your age, your income, or your goals, taxes will figure somehow in your investment choices. What you pay in taxes has a great deal to do with how much money is left for you to spend. Obviously, the less tax you pay, the more money you have.

A word here about tax definitions:

■ Tax-advantaged is a catchall term that can be used to describe practically any kind of investment. It means nothing specific. Salesmen might even use it when there is no tax advantage at also.

■ Tax-deferred means that current taxes are not due on an investment. The money in annuities and cash value life insurance policies enjoys tax deferral on investment earnings. Taxes are not due until the money is withdrawn.

■ Tax-free means that no taxes are due *ever* on that investment. That is the case for some types of municipal bonds issued by state, city or other local governments. Sometimes called "munis," many are also free of state and local taxes.

■ Pre-tax means that you may use money for some purpose before you pay tax on it. Sometimes you never pay tax on it. That's the case with money you spend on certain health care or dependent care needs. You are also permitted to use pre-tax money for certain retirement accounts like a 401(k). In this case, tax will be due when you take the money out.

Deferring taxes on money you put away for retirement can be a big advantage. The 401(k) plan is not the only plan that allows you to defer taxes. IRAs also permit you to put money away without a bite for taxes, where it can grow until retirement. If you need to make a choice between the two, you should understand some pros and cons of each.

How should you decide between a 401(k) plan and an IRA? The 401(k) plan is more attractive in almost every case. The most obvious reason to choose the 401(k) plan is that most plans provide an employer match. If yours does, the 401(k) plan is clearly the best choice. A 401(k) plan also allows you to contribute more—$16,500 if you are forty-nine years old or below, $22,000 if you are fifty or above. That compares to $5,000 for the IRA for taxpayers forty-nine and below and $6,000 for those fifty and above.

So even if your employer does not provide a match, there are reasons to go with the 401(k) plan, provided it has good investment options. Saving is practically painless: Regular deductions are made from each paycheck, eliminating the trouble of deciding whether or not to invest. That helps you take advantage of dollar-cost averaging (p. 156 offers to a more detailed section on dollar-cost averaging), a superior method of investing that allows you to buy more shares of your mutual fund when the market is down, less when it is up.

Finally, a 401(k) plan is what the government refers to as a "tax-qualified plan." When Congress makes pension rules, the rules are often different for qualified plans and for other types of retirement plans. Additionally, in 1996 Congress passed a law allowing those who continue to work past age 70½ to put off mandatory withdrawals on their retirement accounts, which, for retired taxpayers, must begin at age 70½. This rule, too, applies only to qualified plans, not to IRAs. The money in a qualified plan can be rolled into a similar plan at another employer. And the assets in a qualified plan are protected in bankruptcy. In many states, IRA assets do not have that protection.

There are different rules for getting the money out, too. Withdrawing money from either plan before age 59½ usually means you must pay a 10 percent penalty. You can withdraw the money in an IRA if you are willing to pay the penalty. But you cannot withdraw money from a 401(k) plan unless you qualify for stringent hardship withdrawal rules. On the other hand, most 401(k) plans permit loans for almost any reason. You cannot borrow from your IRA.

12

What about Roth?

MOST U.S. ADMINISTRATIONS understand the urgency of retirement savings for Americans. But no two take the same view of it. Some believe the government should provide much more for retirees; some much less. And at the beginning of 2009, after 401(k) participants lost big chunks of retirement money in the stock market, there was a movement to get rid of 401(k) plans altogether.[1]

As a result, each major tax reform act addresses retirement savings in some way: by raising the limit on retirement savings contributions or lowering it; or by taking away tax advantages or giving more of them. So the tax code for retirement savings is convoluted and complex, just as it is for most other taxable events.

One of the provisions of the Taxpayer Relief Act of 1997 created the Roth IRA, named for Senator William Roth of Delaware, a long-time campaigner for retirement accounts, and the Roth IRA became available beginning in 1998. The twist to a Roth account is that you contribute after-tax money and the earnings on it grow tax free so that you need never pay tax on that money again. For 2008, individuals are limited to contributing no more than $5,000 to a Roth IRA if under age fifty and $6,000 if age fifty or older. Roth IRAs also have an income ceiling: They are prohibited when taxpayers earn a modified gross income of more than $110,000 or $160,000 for married filing jointly.

The Roth 401(k) account was added to the family in 2006. It combines some of the most advantageous aspects of both the 401(k) plan and the Roth IRA. Under the Roth 401(k) plan, employees can contribute funds on a post-tax elective deferral basis, in addition to, or instead of, pre-tax elective deferrals under their traditional 401(k) plans.

---

1. See "The Plot to Kill the 401(k)" in *Plan Sponsor* magazine, December 2008, online at http://www.plansponsor.com/magazine_type3/?RECORD_ID=42562.

An employee's combined elective deferrals—whether to a traditional 401(k) plan, a Roth 401(k) plan, or to both—cannot exceed $16,500 for tax year 2009 if a participant is under age fifty; if the employee is older than fifty, she may contribute $22,000. Employer matching funds must be made on a pre-tax basis. They cannot be made into the designated Roth account and cannot receive Roth tax treatment.

Here are some big advantages to the Roth:

1. Withdrawals from the account are completely tax-free. Tax payers who can leave the money untouched for a long period of time can do better with this open-ended savings vehicle.

2. There is no mandatory withdrawal schedule. You need never take the money out during your lifetime. It can continue to grow tax-deferred. If you live to be eighty or ninety or one hundred, you don't have to take anything out and you can keep contributing as long as you earn an income.

3. There is no 10 percent penalty made on early withdrawals before age 59½ provided you withdraw the contributions you made, not the earnings. That means your money is not out of reach until retirement.

4. You can continue to contribute to the account as long as you continue to earn employment income. With the traditional IRA, you cannot contribute after age 70½.

5. The money is not included in taxable income when you withdraw it. That can be important, for example, for those who receive Social Security income. Money from a traditional IRA is included in taxable income, which can make Social Security benefits taxable for some people.

These advantages mean that if a Roth is available to you, you should consider it carefully.

13

Contribute, Contribute

NAVIGATING THE EMPLOYMENT landscape today is tough. The financial meltdown of 2008 and the recessionary economy of 2009 make it tougher still. We need plenty of ingenuity to figure out how to make a living, hone skills, build a resume and juggle financial needs. All investors took a hit in the markets of 2008 and early 2009 and it seemed that the 401(k) plan was just another cause for distress. I see that. But I don't believe that abandoning your 401(k) plan will make your future brighter. A 401(k) plan can still help you build an asset base that you otherwise wouldn't have; it can still help create financial independence.

Too many people still fail to use it. Eligible 401(k) investors could be walking away from an estimated $1,000 a year in free 401(k) money, according to Pam Hess, head of retirement services for Hewitt Associates. Nearly 47 percent of eligible American workers either fail to participate in their company's 401(k) plan or don't invest enough to take full advantage of free matching contributions from their employers, which are typically fifty cents on every dollar contributed to a certain percentage of salary, often 6 percent. So if you contribute 6 percent of your salary, your employer might contribute 50 cents for each dollar, or another 3 percent of your salary. Hess arrived at the $1,000 figure by assuming the match is roughly 3 percent of salary; the average salary is $33,350.

Younger employees and those at lower salary levels are least likely to contribute. Yet these are the employees who can profit most from a 401(k) plan. The 401(k) plan is a better bet than a traditional pension for a younger worker. There is a heavy tilt in favor of younger people in these plans. That's because of the time value of money. The contribution is the same but a young person has so much longer to allow the dollars to compound so that he doesn't have to save as much to get to the same place.

The 401(k) plan is great for job hoppers because the plans are portable. When you leave your job, the money is yours. You can roll it into an IRA, leave it with your employer—in an account in your name of course—or move it to your new employer's 401(k) plan. You can even use it to tide you through a rough spot if you feel desperate. Don't plan to use your retirement nest egg early; knowing you have money set aside might help you to feel more confident in taking risks to move ahead.

If the 401(k) plan is better for younger workers and job hoppers, it follows that the traditional pension serves the older worker better—a subject we discussed in Part One. An employee would get the optimal pension benefit by working the first half of his career under a defined contribution plan like a 401(k) plan and the second half with a rich traditional defined benefit plan. Planning your career based on your pension benefits would be a big mistake if it meant spending your life doing unsatisfying work. But if the pension benefit was most important, that would be the way to do it.

Consider the pension benefits of four employees, each with a final salary of $150,000. The first, who spent his thirty-year career at a company with a traditional defined benefit pension, retires with an annual benefit of $67,500. The employee who spent the first fifteen years with a company with a 401(k) plan and the second with the defined benefit plan would have $74,110. The other two workers—the one who spent an entire career with a 401(k) plan and the one who spent the first half of his career with defined benefit plan and second with 401(k) plan did worse.

What's at work here is the power of compounding on money tucked away in the early years combined with a benefit based on the fatter salary of the later years. The message is a simple one: Contribute whatever you can to a 401(k) plan as early as possible, even if you start with just a few dollars a month. If your employer provides any type of match, contribute up to the limit to capture it. This is one of the most important things you can do to establish your financial independence.

Don't let the fresh memory of the market crash in 2008–09 determine your future—that's what will happen if you drop out of the 401(k). Instead, learn this lesson: If you can member the unhappy surprises on both the upside and the downside, it will be easier to stay on course.

14

Protecting Your Income

WHAT DOES DISABILITY insurance have to do with a book on 401(k) plans? A good deal. Your income—and your ability to keep bringing it in and enhancing it—is your single biggest asset. So the biggest threat to you is an illness or accident that would cut off that income.

If you are a man over thirty-five, there is one chance in five that you will be disabled and unable to work before you retire, according to the National Association of Insurance Commissioners. A thirty-five-year-old woman faces a nearly one-in-three risk of disability lasting at least ninety days before reaching retirement.

You need health insurance to pay medical bills. And you need disability income insurance to keep income coming. Many employees assume that they have adequate coverage through their employee benefit plan and that they don't need to buy an individual policy. But at least 75 percent of American companies do not provide disability policies, while those who do usually provide a short-term policy to tide you over for a period of days or weeks.

If you buy an individual disability policy and pay the premiums, your benefits will be tax-free. If your employer pays the premiums, benefits are taxable. To buy disability insurance, you must prove that you are in good health and that you have an income. Don't wait until you need it. You may not qualify.

What should you look for? Policies are both complex and expensive: the more complex, the more expensive. "There are a lot of bells and whistles on disability policies that significantly increase the premium amount," says Michael J. Chasnoff, a financial planner in Cincinnati. "Too often people buy features that they are unaware of that add a lot to the premium."

Cost-of-living adjustments can add 50 percent to the premium—a nice feature, to be sure, but perhaps not affordable. Focus on getting the highest possible monthly benefit. "Get high basic coverage and leave out some of the extras," says Glenn S. Daily, an insurance consultant in New York and author of *The Individual Investor's Guide to Low-Load Insurance Products*.

When you shop for a policy, check the following:

■ **The waiting period.** This is comparable to a deductible on a medical plan. The longer you wait before drawing benefits, the lower the premium. The waiting period ranges from 30 days to 180 days and more. Most financial planners recommend a 90-day waiting period. That means you would start collecting benefits four months after you are disabled—the 90-day wait and another 30 days before the insurer writes the check.

■ **The benefit period.** You can buy a policy that will pay benefits for one, two, or five years, until you reach age sixty-five, or for your lifetime. Most advisors suggest age sixty-five. Lifetime coverage is extremely expensive.

■ **Income replacement.** Look for a benefit that would replace 60 to 70 percent of your total compensation. If you earn $100,000, your policy should pay $60,000. Remember that no tax will be due on your benefit.

I believe that consumers will become even more cost conscious about financial products in 2010 and beyond. They must. We all need to protect ourselves from the most devastating losses. But insurance policies, often misunderstood, give us an opportunity to cover what could be devastating losses and still save money by sholding the more predictable losses ourselves.

PART TWO

401(к) PLAN BASICS

Planning for the Future

The 401(k) plan did not start a workplace revolution, yet it is representative of myriad changes that affect every worker in America. If we could name the result, we might call it the end of paternalism, the era when Americans expected an employer to act as watchful parent, taking care that all a worker's needs be met once he'd left home and taken a job. If he became ill, injured, got married, or had a baby, or if a family member died, the employer would be there to offer comfort and help. Of course, this employee–employer relationship faded with the growth of a global economy. But some of us refuse to believe that; we deny the fact that our employer is not a parent, is not responsible for any of us.

Do you ever stop in an office or at a store or restaurant and hear an employee say: "No one appreciates me around here. If I was gone, then they'd see how much they needed me." Perhaps it's not unusual to want validation from an employer ("Nice job") or an offer for a bonus or salary increase. But when these niceties become part of the expected compensation package as they did on Wall Street by the end of 2008, the system is broken. When taxpayers suffering from job loss, debt, and a lack of funds to send their kids to college are asked to bail out banks and insurers who continue to use corporate jets and host employee retreats that cost hundreds of thousands of dollars, the system is broken. "Employees" have overestimated their value.

Consider Robert Rubin, former Treasury secretary, former head of Goldman Sachs, and a consultant and member of the board of directors at Citibank. When Citibank teetered close to failure, the *Wall Street Journal* asked Rubin how he could justify collecting millions of dollars in compensation for overseeing the bank's implosion. Well, Rubin said, plenty of other companies wanted to hire him and would have been happy to pay much more. Or consider John Thain's position as head of Merrill Lynch when that company was saved from disintegration in a takeover from Bank of America. Thain argued that he still deserved his $10 million year-end bonus because he'd done better than some of the other brokerages. Which ones? Merrill lost $15.31 billion in the fourth quarter. On the other hand, the *New York Times* wrote about a group of restaurant workers who offered to work a free shift for the restaurant's owner because of the tight economy. The owner had put his money in the till to meet payroll in the past, and they wanted to help out, too.

We read a lot about employer discrimination and about the lawsuits filed to protest it. But we read less about employees who go too far to get their "fair share" so that it is much more than their fair share. I once received a letter from a man in Georgia who wrote to complain of the way his wife's employer had mistreated her. She worked many years in a corporate position for a large company. When she heard rumors that the company was planning to cut back its work force, she found another job with a six-figure income. Shortly after she started her new job, her former employer did downsize, offering generous severance packages to those in her former department. This man reasoned that his wife had been cheated out of money that was hers. This couple contacted the former employer as well as a lawyer but was unable to get a severance package for the wife. When he saw that I was writing about severance packages and the like, he thought I would be sympathetic and perhaps be able to help. He was wrong.

This guy is a great example of someone heading off in the wrong direction. The longer he and his wife continue to spend their energy on getting angry and trying to correct something that they perceive as unfair, the further behind they will be. And imagine how tired their friends will get of hearing about it! The workplace has become treacherous. You need all your wits and your energy to do a good job and set a course for yourself. One good thing about the Great Depression was that people pulled together and helped each other out. I also like to think that people who got work, worked hard. I do know that lots of people were "hardly working" at the beginning of the twenty-first century. If we'd lost something, it was probably pride in our work. So many Americans boasted about earning six-figure incomes for doing practically nothing that those of us who were working hard for much less felt sort of silly about it. If we all learn something from this Great Recession, as it's being called, it would be the joy of earning money by working hard at something we love.

The new employment contract is a short-term, temporary one. In recognition of this, many employers offer to provide skills training so that employees will be more valuable when they move to their next job. The notice might be nothing more than a note on the bulletin board or an item in the company newsletter, announcing courses on presentation skills or computer skills. Find out about anything that could help you grow as an employee or as a person. Take the challenge.

The workplace today offers an opportunity to be a pessimist or to be an optimist. Which will you choose? Is your 401(k) plan a burden or an opportunity? What about your job? Your career? If you've been following along in this book, you've already discovered that the 401(k) plan was not set up to provide an employee bonanza. You can get a lot out of these plans. But you may as well understand that you're not the only one with something at stake. You can get the most out of your 401(k) plan if you understand who is involved and what these players hope to accomplish.

The global economy turned steeply downward in the fall of 2008. The bursting of the housing bubble went well beyond the homeowners who lost their homes to hit those on Wall Street who created the instruments that enabled the risky subprime mortgage market to grow and banks around the world that participated in these financial instruments. What is next is uncertain, except that we know things will be different. Putting the blame on Wall Street, on former President George W. Bush, or on current President Barack Obama will not improve your own situation. This is a lesson I learned when my beautiful six-year-old daughter developed a blinding eye disease. We'd taken her to the doctor regularly. How could this happen? Even when I brought her in because her right eye looked strange to me, the doctor didn't discover that she couldn't see out of it. He didn't check. Every parent who has ever faced a chronic disease with a child knows the emotional turbulence that comes with it, the questioning: How did she deserve this? What did I do wrong?

Americans—indeed, people all over the world—ask this question as the global economy contracts and changes. Industrial production in the United States fell 15 percent in March 2009 from that month a year earlier, according to the Federal Reserve; a survey of manufacturers predicted that the sector would continue to contract for three to six months, or for most of 2009, as reported in the *Wall Street Journal* on April 17, 2009.

Wouldn't it be wonderful to lay the blame on someone else—on banking regulators, for instance? Had the problem of the sick economy been revealed sooner, it would have had a better chance of recovery. Charging the pediatrician with neglect would do absolutely nothing to heal my daughter. In fact, it might encourage the opposite of healing, the rerouting of all the energy I needed to help my daughter and my family into anger at someone whom I decided was to blame. If I were to stay alive, physically, emotionally, mentally, and spiritually, I had to put all the energy I had into our family's healing. I think that's true of our economy now as well.

Americans must make decisions on what their lives will be like going forward. It's time to get creative. Peggy Noonan, a columnist for the *Wall Street Journal*, wrote a story in April 2009, right after tax day, about the Wojtowicz family in Michigan who decided to cut up their credit cards; to eliminate satellite television, high-tech toys and restaurant dining; to live on a forty-acre farm; and to plant a garden, raise chickens and pigs, and install a wood furnace. The story, which first ran in *USA Today*, garnered hundreds of comments from others who said they were making similar decisions. "To some degree the story sounded like the future, or the future as a lot of people are hoping it will be: pared down, more natural, more stable, less full of enervating overstimulation," Noonan wrote.[1]

I doubt if 300 million Americans will go "back to the land." Good thing, too, as the land couldn't support all of us. But this is a good time to think about your future. Help is available everywhere. A section of the *Wall Street Journal* called "Encore" regularly reports on transitions. In April 2009, in a story about community colleges,

---

1. Peggy Noonan, "Goodbye Bland Affluence," *Wall Street Journal*, April 17, 2009, http://online.wsj.com/article/SB123992073614326997.html.

Kelly Greene reported that "the humble community college is turning out to be one of the best resources for older adults seeking new directions—and new jobs—later in life." Greene mentioned new programs across the country, including teacher certification, gerontology certification, training for summer jobs at national parks, as well as help with small-business start-ups. (See Part Five for more information on transitions.) In this section, we'll take a look at 401(k) plan basics.

The Three Main Players

FINANCIAL MISTAKES often result from a lack of perspective. We see the landscape from ground level in the forest. To make sound financial decisions, you should understand who you're dealing with and what vested interests your partners have.

The three players involved in the 401(k) plan are your employer, who sponsors the plan; you and the other employees who participate in the plan (or don't participate); and the government, which regulates the plan, aiming to make certain that employees are treated fairly, that the company doesn't take off with the money, and that the Internal Revenue Service (IRS) eventually gets its money from the plan in the form of taxes.

Each of the three makes demands on the 401(k) plan, and each gets something out of it. Naturally, you're concerned with what you get out of the plan. That will depend a good deal on you and your understanding of the process. Over the years that I've been writing about personal finance, I've received hundreds of letters from readers who made big financial mistakes simply because they misunderstood these rules and mistakenly believed that the entire process is set up to benefit them.

The first 401(k) plan, set up in 1981, was designed almost entirely as a solution for employers who couldn't attract lower-paid workers to a retirement plan. That's because if lower-paid workers don't contribute, the government nixes the plan as a benefit for the higher paid. The carrot to entice lower-paid workers was the company match—the free money that they would otherwise leave on the table.

Under the traditional defined benefit pension plans, which were still the norm at the time, employers were responsible for setting aside all of the money for pensions, for investing it, and for paying it out. It didn't take long for employers to see that providing a company match in a 401(k) would be much cheaper—and involve far less responsibility—than funding the whole pension.

Critics are quick to say that employers have abdicated their responsibility to employees by doing this. I don't agree. The world changes and we must change or be left behind. Still, I've attended a number of conferences and seminars on 401(k) investing where I was offended by the condescending manner in which pension "experts" referred to us, the "little guys." At one, in Palm Beach, Florida, a Yale Law School professor said that the 401(k) plan is a catastrophe because we "little people" don't know how to invest. "Bucky Six-Pack simply doesn't know how to make investment choices," he told the gathered financial professionals. Bucky indeed! The lesson is to take the "experts" with a grain of salt and focus on how to get the most out of your own plan.

The growth of 401(k) plans coincided with a revolution in American business. Bloated companies were looking for ways to trim down, shift costs, and improve their bottom lines. The 401(k) plan offered one solution. Thanks to reduced employee benefit costs, American companies were able to become competitive in the global economy again.

This transition certainly wasn't as smooth as I've presented it. But given the new state of the world, especially since the end of 2008, employees would be foolhardy to expect employers to take up the slack. Today, few employers promise anything. Not surprisingly then, there has been a massive decline in employee loyalty over the past two or three decades. Arguing about whether it is right or wrong for your company to take care of you now and in retirement will not do us much good. We may as well be pragmatic about it and make the best use we can of the situation we're in.

The tacit contract between workers and employers, if one still exists, has changed dramatically. This is a time of fewer promotions, smaller raises, just-in-time inventory, more workforce reductions, and increased employee responsibility for retirement. We will be much better off in our work and our personal lives if we use this to our advantage.

What Your Employer Wants

MOST EMPLOYERS WHO USE 401(k) plans want to offer a good plan. They realize that employees have more responsibilities for their own financial needs today, and they want them to succeed. On the other hand, they do not want to be on the hook if the employees fail to save enough.

So employers attempt to achieve a delicate balance. They know that novice investors tend to put too little into the stock market and too much into guaranteed investments like guaranteed investment contracts (GICs). But they are afraid to advise employees to move to stocks to improve their returns for fear the employees will lose money and blame them, or worse yet, sue them. The dismal market returns in 2008 fed these fears.

The government gets involved here, too, and mandates that the employer observe certain "fairness" rules and regulations. There are two basic types of 401(k) plans. The first requires the employer take fiduciary responsibility for acting in the best interest of employees. It can offer any choice of investment options. But the employer who chooses this plan faces liability if employees lose money because of bad investment decisions.

The second type of 401(k) plan relieves the employer of fiduciary responsibility provided it complies with certain rules. These rules, which are referred to as 404(c) regulations, were finalized in 1992 and spell out what an employer must do if it wants limited liability protection when participants direct the investment of their own accounts, according to Kyle Brown, retirement counsel at Watson Wyatt in Washington.

Employers who choose to comply with these regulations must offer at least three diversified investment choices with a wide variety of risk/return characteristics, allow the employee to shift investments at least every three months, disclose options, and provide some sort of communication/education. Employer stock can be offered, but because it is not a diversified investment, it does not qualify as one of the three choices.

Employers who comply will not be liable in the event of losses from bad investment decisions. But they will still be on the hook for a broad range of things like picking investment managers and making certain the options offered are good ones.

These loose rules allow a huge range of possibilities. The guidelines do not mean every 401(k) plan is a good one. Consider how two companies who set up their 401(k) plans in the 1990s went about meeting their responsibilities.

When Morningstar, the Chicago company that made its reputation by rating mutual funds, set up a plan in 1991, it selected one top-notch fund in each asset class, such as a U.S large company fund, a U.S. small company fund, a money market fund, an international stock fund, and a natural resource fund for those employees who wanted an inflation hedge. Morningstar made it easy for employees to set up their 401(k) plans because each fund is a good one and is distinct from the others. In other words, each fund represented an asset class such as international stock or commodities or bonds rather than offering several "name brand" funds that are indistinguishable from one another. A Morningstar employee need only consider which asset classes he or she wants to include, such as U.S. large companies, and pick the fund from that class.

General Motors (GM) took the opposite approach. In 1995, GM had the largest 401(k) in the country with $12 billion in assets but just a handful of sleepy investment options. The automaker knew it needed to increase investment options but was apparently unwilling to go the route of Morningstar and put an implicit stamp of approval on a handful of funds.

Instead, GM offered a complex plan with thirty-seven choices. Predictably, many employees felt overwhelmed. "The GM plan just got better," an engineer at the company told me at the time. "But it also got a lot more complicated and I don't have time to do it on my own." Like hundreds of other employees, this engineer hired a broker to manage his 401(k) account for a fee. Putting your account in the hands of a broker opens a new can of worms including the conflicts of interest the broker might have as well as the cost of fees.

What the Government Wants

WHY DOES THE GOVERNMENT always get involved in these stories? For a couple of reasons. First, the government loses billions of dollars in taxes each year because the dollars deposited into 401(k) plans have not yet been taxed. When tax reformers limited the availability of IRAs in the Tax Reform Act of 1986, they raised tax revenues by closing what some lawmakers viewed as a loophole for the "rich."

The second reason is an obvious one: Whenever Congress looks for a way to raise revenue, tax-deferred investments and tax-free investments get a close examination. That's what happened in 2009 as the Obama Administration looked for ways to solve the economy's collapse and raise revenue for the new programs it hoped to start. As Congress casts about looking for more tax revenue, nothing is sacred. There was buzz in early 2009 about eliminating, or seriously reducing, tax advantages for 401(k) plans. Most experts believe that's history now. The 401(k) plan, like the tax deduction for interest paid on a mortgage for a primary residence, has strong support from middle-class Americans. "They can tinker with the edges, but the 401(k) plan is here to stay," says Kyle Brown, counsel for retirement at Watson Wyatt in Washington.

Still, the Internal Revenue Service (IRS) keeps a close eye on how the plans are set up and maintained to make sure no additional taxes are lost. And Congress makes rules on when and how the money is withdrawn so that the government will eventually collect these lost tax dollars.

The Department of Labor is another player on the government team. Labor gets involved because 401(k) plans permit employers to provide part of employee compensation in the form of benefits rather than straight salary dollars in a paycheck. The Department of Labor wants to be certain that the money employees receive as benefits gets ample protection.

Like traditional pension plans, 401(k) plans are "qualified plans," which means that they qualify for preferential tax treatment. In the case of the 401(k) plans, all of the advantages we've been talking about give participants preferential tax treatment: Participants are permitted to contribute money before they pay tax on it. And employers, too, are permitted to make matching pre-tax contributions.

Qualified plans must obey strict guidelines if they are to maintain this special tax status. Plans at private companies must follow strict rules outlined in the tax code and the Employee Retirement Income Security Act of 1974, or ERISA. The rules govern participation, vesting schedules and nondiscrimination testing. They are enforced by the Department of Labor, the IRS, and the Treasury Department.

In addition to making certain that it gets its tax dollars eventually, the government wants to be certain that those tax dollars it gives up—at least temporarily—are used to benefit a broad range of employees, not just the highly paid executives who are setting up the plan. That's where the participation, vesting schedules, and nondiscrimination rules come in. To "qualify," a plan must prove that it provides benefits for all workers.

The government puts teeth in its regulations, too. A 401(k) plan that does not comply with all the rules can lose its special tax-qualified status or be "disqualified," a word that strikes fear in the hearts of employers and benefits consultants who design these plans. If a plan is disqualified, the sponsor, or employer who sponsors the plan, loses his tax deduction for all the contributions it has made. The employer must pay back taxes and penalties on the unpaid tax. Not only is this expensive, but "cheating" employees on their 401(k) benefits makes for bad publicity.

Disqualification would be bad news for participants, too, as it means they now owe taxes on all the money they have contributed to the plan. Tax lawyers and consultants call this the "big stick," referring to the punishment for employers who fail to comply. That threat makes employers eager to adhere to the rules laid down for qualified plans. It pays for you, too, to understand these rules.

How to Use This Stuff

A 401(k) PLAN is certainly not as good as an inheritance. However, contrary to what a lot of critics say, it can be better than a traditional defined benefit pension where your employer foots the entire bill. The defined benefit plans sounds promising, but unless you spend your working career at one company, the results are likely to be disappointing.

And defined benefit plans can enslave workers. For every worker who retires fulfilled from a happy career at one employer, there might be a dozen who felt forced to stick with their employer—no matter how unsatisfying—because of pension requirements. That became clear to me one day as I headed into New York on an Amtrak train after a freak spring snowstorm delayed the train for five hours. Once the passengers realized they would never make it to their meetings and all the food and drinks in the snack car disappeared, tension gave way to a sort of camaraderie. People spilled their life stories.

The man in the seat behind me confided to his seatmate that he had taken early retirement at age sixty after thirty-one years as an engineer with the same company. He didn't have enough income to retire and knew he had to find work. Yet "it was almost a relief to be forced to make a change," he said. "I was so bored there for all those years." He got good assignments and tackled each one with enthusiasm but six months of interesting work was followed by three or four or five years of complete boredom.

This man was one of the "lucky employees," we read about—the worker of yesteryear who had lifetime employment. In fact, this man told his new friend, he had counseled his two daughters, who were in their thirties, to plan a career of job hopping, adding to their skills by both formal education and by working at different companies.

A 401(k) plan can be a great tool for a job hopper because it can buy you the freedom that my fellow Amtrak passenger lost in his career. You can also turn the plan to your advantage. Consider that your employer wants you to participate. If you are a lower-paid worker—that means any salary under $110,000 in 2009—your employer *really* wants you to participate. That's because if workers under this income level don't participate, the higher-paid employees can't contribute as much.

Remember the government's agenda? The government wants to make certain that 401(k) plans are not designed as a plum for the top executives. One of the ways it does that is to set up tests to make certain the plans do not discriminate in favor of the highly paid and against the rank and file.

To prove it is nondiscriminatory, the plan must pass certain tests. First, it must be available to a broad group of employees. It may exclude, for example, union employees covered under a collective bargaining agreement if retirement benefits are a part of that agreement. It may also exclude employees who do not meet minimum eligibility requirements of age and length of service, nonresident aliens, and, of course, those who are terminated.

But plans must undergo broad tests to make certain they don't benefit only key employees. To perform this test, which is called the "actual deferral percentage test," employees are split into two groups, those who earn under $110,000 and those who earn over $110,000. Those in the higher-income group can contribute on average, just 2 percent more than the average contributed by the lower-income group.

So employers want "lower-paid" workers to contribute as much as possible, up to the legal limit of $16,500 for employees age forty-nine and younger and $22,000 for those fifty and older for 2009. The more the lower-paid group contributes as a percent of pay, the more the higher-paid group can contribute. If an employer elects to use the automatic deferral option implemented beginning in 2008, the employer need not perform the nondiscrimination test. Under automatic deferral, the employer automatically enrolls new employees in the plan unless they decide to opt out. This provision became available in 2006. The rule outlines the requirements for automatically enrolling new employees in the plan where they become eligible. For more information on automatic enrolled see p. 94.

5

The Limit

REMEMBER THAT THE U.S. GOVERNMENT, via Congress, keeps a tab on how much money escapes current taxes. In the fall of 2008, the House education and labor committees held a hearing about whether 401(k) plans should be retired as a thirty-year experiment that ended in failure when everyone lost money in the stock market crash. One speaker said the government should offer a different kind of retirement plan for Americans, one run by the government.

Prior to the 1986 Tax Reform Act, participants were permitted to put a great deal of money into their 401(k) plans—up to $30,000 a year. But that tax reform law, which limited or eliminated many types of tax shelters, reduced as well the amount that individuals could contribute to their 401(k) plans, to $7,000 in 1987, an amount set to increase with inflation. A 1994 law decreed that the limit would rise only in $500 increments. When inflation is low, the limit may remain the same for two years. A later ruling set different limits for those younger than forty-nine and those older than fifty.

The limit for participants younger than forty-nine is $16,500 for 2009. For participants age fifty and over, the limit is $22,000. For many employees, a more important limitation is the one imposed by the actual derferral percentage (ADP) test. This test, which is typically called a nondiscrimination test, is mandated by the government to determine that the plan is not unfairly favoring its higher-paid workers. To comply with government rules, 401(k) plans must pass the test for each plan year.

The 2006 Pension Protection Act added a "safe harbor" that said a plan that had automatic deferral for lower-paid workers beginning at 3 percent when they began employment, increasing to 4 percent a year later, and then increasing again to 5 percent and 6 percent after the third year and beyond, is not required to test for nondiscrimination.

This law, was intended to bring more lower-paid workers into the plan, and it has. Employers must explain the plan to new employees and give them the option to opt out or to get their money back after the first two paychecks if they want to opt out. This rule became effective for the 2008 plan year after the Department of Labor issued guidance on the appropriate default investment for this money. The Department of Labor declared balanced funds and target-date funds to be appropriate. A balanced fund is one that includes both stocks and bonds, usually weighted a bit toward stocks. Target-date funds offer a choice of retirement dates such as 2020, 2030, and so forth. The portfolio is then managed using a "glide path," or an increasingly conservative mix of asset classes as the target date approaches.

For employers who must administer the nondiscrimination test, here's how it works: Contributions made by employees earning less than $110,000 in 2009—the number is indexed—are tossed into a pool to determine the average percentage of salaries they contribute to the 401(k) account. Then the average salary contribution is calculated for those earning more than $110,000. The Department of Labor mandates that the spread between the two groups be regulated: In most cases, it is limited to 2 percentage points. If the group that is not highly compensated contributes 4 percent of salary on average, the highly compensated group can contribute no more than 6 percent on average.

Suppose a company discovers that its highly compensated executives are contributing an average of 7 percent and its lower-paid group only 4 percent. In the past, the company was forced to return the excess dollars as taxable income to the higher-paid group. The 2006 Pension Protection Act allows employers to conduct the test using the prior year's numbers. An employer would be delighted if a fifty-five-year-old employee in the lower-income group earning $109,000 contributed the full $22,000, or 20 percent of her salary, because that would boost the average for the lower-paid group and allow the higher-paid group to contribute more.

Section 415 of the Internal Revenue Code imposes a limit on total non-taxable savings made by and for an employee. This includes the deferral limits just discussed as well as employee after-tax contributions, the employer match, and any other employer contributions such as profit-sharing. The combination of all these contributions cannot exceed the lesser of 100 percent of income or $49,000 for 2009.

What Is Vesting?

VESTING REFERS to the ownership of the money in your retirement plan and can mean different things depending on the style of the plan. In a pension plan, if you quit your job or are terminated before becoming entirely vested, you can't collect any of the money set aside in your retirement fund. When you are entirely vested, retirement benefits must be paid to you, even if you leave the company years before retirement. If you return to a former employer after a "break in service," or after working somewhere else, you must be given credit for your prior service.

Many employers see vesting as a way to reward loyal employees for sticking with the company and as a way to keep employees on board. But under traditional defined benefit pensions, vesting by itself does not mean much in the way of benefits. Even an employee who had worked ten years for a company—say from age twenty-two to age thirty-two—might have very little in the way of vested benefits, certainly not enough to turn down a good career opportunity.

A 401(k) plan functions differently from a defined benefit pension plan. The money an employee contributes to a 401(k) plan is vested immediately. Whenever that employee leaves the employer, he has the right to take that money with him. But the money an employer contributes to the account—the company match or profit-sharing dollars—is a different category, controlled by the employer.

An employer *may* provide immediate vesting on that money, too. But it is more likely to use a scaled vesting schedule that dictates how long an employee must work in order to have ownership of the company match. Employers may provide vesting in one year or two years, but they are not permitted to establish vesting schedules that go beyond the maximum periods set forth in section 411 of the Internal

Revenue Code. These guidelines, which were revised in 2008, permit two choices: three-year "cliff vesting" or two-to-six-year "graduated vesting".

Under cliff vesting, the employee is not vested in any of the employer's contribution until he completes three years of service. Then he is immediately 100 percent vested in all employer contributions. If he leaves after that point, the money belongs to him. Under graduated vesting, the employee becomes invested in 20 percent of the employer contribution after two years, 40 percent after three years, 60 percent after four years, 80 percent after five years, and 100 percent in six years.

It is probably not worth your while to stick with an employer to become vested in a traditional pension plan, particularly if you are young. Benefits in these pensions are heavily weighted toward older, higher-paid employees. If you've been working only five years, you may have earned a few hundred dollars to be paid forty-some years from now.

But with your 401(k) plan, it becomes easy to see what you gain by waiting until you're vested in the plan. Suppose your employer matches 50 percent of your contribution up to 6 percent of your salary, and the account operates under a three-year cliff-vesting period. You earn $80,000 and contribute the full 6 percent, or $4,800 per year. Your employer contributes 50 percent, or $2,400 per year. After three years, your employer's contribution totals $7,200 *plus* the earnings on that money. If you leave after two and a half years, you leave all that money on the table.

That shouldn't be enough money to persuade you to give up a great career move, but it's certainly enough to deserve your attention. One of the great benefits of 401(k) plans is that they are portable. Even if you work for half a dozen different employers, you can still earn the same benefits that you might have earned working for just one. Check your company's vesting schedule and keep it in mind when planning your career.

Qualifying Rules

EMPLOYERS WHO SPONSOR 401(K) plans must observe certain rules on when employees can participate in a company plan. Employers are permitted to impose two eligibility requirements. The first is called the "year of service requirement." It allows the employer to say that you must work for the company for a certain period of time before you are allowed to participate in the plan. But that time period cannot be more than one year. The exception to this is if an employer offers complete vesting at the end of two years of service.

The employer is also permitted to say that participants must be a certain age before contributing, but the maximum age the employer is permitted to specify is twenty-one. In combination with time constraints, an employer may say you must be nineteen years old and work for the company for six months before you can contribute to the plan, or that you must be twenty years old and work for the company for one year. In any case, the employer may not require contributors to be older than twenty-one or have a waiting period longer than one year. An exception to the rule is that educational institutions may limit participation until age twenty-six, according to Kyle Brown of Watson Wyatt benefit consultants.

A year of service is calculated as a twelve-month period beginning on the first day of employment during which an employee works at least 1,000 hours, which is roughly a twenty-hour workweek. If an employee begins work on January 1 but does not work 1,000 hours by December 31, a new period begins again on January 1.

So an employee who continues to work part-time and under 1,000 hours a year need not be covered by the employer's 401(k) plan. Once an employee works 1,000 hours in a year and satisfies the minimum age and service requirements, though, he must be permitted to participate in the plan at the earliest of the following dates: either the first day of the plan year that begins after he has become eligible, or six months after the date on which he has become eligible.

Once an employee qualifies for participation, he may ask the employer to withhold a certain portion of his salary to be contributed to the 401(k) retirement plan. These are the pre-tax contributions that 401(k) plans are best known for. A 401(k) plan is actually part of a profit-sharing or stock-bonus plan that includes what is called a cash or deferred arrangement or CODA. Remember the bonus plans that were the precursor of the modern 401(k) plan? Like them, the 401(k) plan permits the employee to ask the employer to defer a portion of his salary rather than give it to him in cash. Many 401(k) plans also allow employees to contribute additional after-tax money that will earn interest on an after-tax basis.

In addition, most plans provide for an employer match, which must be completely nondiscriminatory. For instance, the employer might contribute fifty cents for every dollar contributed by an employee (totaling up to 4 percent of that person's pay). Finally, the employer may decide to make profit-sharing contributions. These are separate from the match and are based on the company's profitability and laid out in the formula. The 401(k) or CODA portion of the plan is only the elective salary deferral. But people often use "401(k)" to refer to the whole plan.

Once an employee qualifies for participation in the company's 401(k) plan, contributions can come from four sources. The first and most common is employee pre-tax contributions, which the employee asks the employer to withhold from pay and to contribute to the plan. The second is employee after-tax contributions. Third and fourth, the employer may make matching contributions as well as discretionary profit-sharing contributions.

Hardship Withdrawal

WITH ALL THE ADVANTAGES of a 401(k) plan, why would anyone who is eligible pass one up? Surveys show that many employees simply don't understand how the plans work. But the main reason that employees don't contribute is because they don't want to lock their money up until retirement. We all have many demands on our money, and we are all more cautious after the beating the markets took in 2008 and 2009. Some of these demands are so pressing it's hard to see a way to squeeze out savings for the future. Sure, setting aside money for retirement is admirable, but many employees feel they simply can't spare a dime.

Indeed, the money you put in your 401(k) plan is locked up. The regulations say that the pre-tax money you contribute cannot be distributed until one of these things happens: you reach age 59½, you leave the company, you become disabled, you die, the plan is terminated, or the employer that sponsors the plan is sold.

Employers and the government realize that this inflexibility is a major hurdle to participation for many employees, particularly younger employees and those who earn less. To combat this, many employers have done what they can to make the money more accessible by exploiting the few exceptions to these tough rules. One is the hardship withdrawal, which outlines circumstances under which you are permitted to withdraw money from your plan.

Your plan is not required to provide for hardship withdrawals. If it does, it must adhere to the government's rules for them. Your employer is responsible for determining whether you in fact have a pressing financial need, or what the Internal Revenue Service (IRS) calls "an immediate and heavy financial need." Your employer must also be satisfied that you have used your other resources and that a withdrawal from your 401(k) account is necessary to fulfill that need.

Six circumstances might make you eligible for a hardship withdrawal. They include the following:

- Medical expenses for you, your spouse or your dependents

- Tuition and other fees for the coming year of college for you, your spouse, your children, or your dependents

- Money for a down payment on your principle residence

- Money to prevent eviction from or foreclosure on your principle home

- Burial or funeral expenses for your parents, your spouse, your children, or your dependents

- Repair for damage to your principal residence

Of course, just because you are buying a home or going to college doesn't mean you qualify for a hardship withdrawal. You must have exhausted every other means of paying for those needs, including taking a loan from your 401(k) plan. You should be prepared to fully document your financial need to your employer.

So the hardship withdrawal doesn't look so good? It gets worse. Once you've cleared all these hurdles and you get the money from your plan, you must pay tax on it as well as a 10 percent penalty for early withdrawal. And you will be barred from making contributions to your plan for one year.

These stiff requirements make hardship withdrawal a last resort. Taking a loan from your plan is far more attractive than making a hardship withdrawal. Most plans allow you to take a loan for any reason, with no questions asked. There is no tax due on the money, and you pay yourself interest, which goes into your 401(k) account.

9

Information about Your Plan

YOU ARE ENTITLED to find out about how your plan works. Under the Employee Retirement Income and Security Act, or ERISA, each 401(k) plan administrator is required to file a summary plan description with the Department of Labor. Your employer is also required under ERISA to make the summary plan description available to plan participants. Each 401(k) plan participant must receive a copy of this booklet, which describes the plan in simple language, no more than ninety days after becoming a plan participant.

Your employer must provide an updated booklet every five years that includes all amendments and other changes to the plan. Some plan sponsors provide only what is legally required in this document, making it pretty dry reading. But others have chosen to use it as a basic communications tool, beefing up the information required by the government to supply additional information about the plan.

However your employer uses it, the booklet is one source of information that *must* be provided to you. It must convey certain basic information in a manner that can be understood by the average participant. And it must include technical information that you might need, such as the names of the trustee and administrator. It must also outline your legal rights.

Although you probably will not sit down with this document to read it cover to cover, you should know what it contains and keep it in a safe place with the other information from your 401(k) plan.

The items that summary description must include are shown in the following box.

Employers are also required to provide a quarterly statement and to allow a change in the election for investments at least quarterly, says Brown. "In my plan, I can change daily."

Summary Plan Description should include the following:

- The plan's name
- The employer's name and address
- An employer identification number or EIN, which is similar to your own Social Security number and identifies your employer with the government
- The plan number
- Type of plan (A 401(k) plan is a defined contribution plan.)
- Type of administration
- The name, address, and telephone number of the plan administrator
- The identity of the plan's lawyer
- Eligibility requirements
- A statement that outlines provisions in collective bargaining agreements that might pertain to the plan
- The plan's fiscal year
- Sources of contributions and the method used to calculate the amount of these contributions
- The plan's termination provisions
- Claim and remedy procedures for participants
- A statement of the ERISA rights of participants

10

Is My Plan Safe?

AS THE MONEY in 401(k) plans has mushroomed, many participants have asked questions about plan safety. In the late 1990s, there was a rash of stories in the press about employers who dipped into 401(k) accounts to pay their own bills and others who simply kept the money they withheld from employee paychecks and used it for their own purposes. Those incidents, which were rare in the first place, are mostly behind us now, says Kyle Brown, retirement counsel at Watson Wyatt.

But still, many employees called 401(k) plan hotlines when the stock market collapsed. In the fourth quarter of 2008, calls to Hewitt Associates, benefits consultants in Lincolnshire, Illinois, increased by 20 percent, according to Pam Hess, director of retirement research. Some plan participants who had money invested in the Lehman Brothers bond index wanted to know if their investment was affected by the collapse of Lehman Brothers. The answer was no, because the index is simply a benchmark for bonds much like the Dow Jones Industrial Average is for stocks.

Most employers are eager to follow all the 401(k) plan rules. The contributions you make to a 401(k) plan are held in a trust. Your employer cannot touch that money, nor can his creditors if he files for bankruptcy. The people and companies that have decision-making authority over the plan are fiduciaries, which means they must always act on behalf of the plan in an informed, prudent manner.

Each plan has a trustee who is responsible for collecting the money, investing it, and paying it out. The plan also has an administrator or record keeper who keeps track of the money and checks for compliance with various government regulations. You can learn more about the people and institutions responsible for safeguarding your 401(k) money in the summary plan document.

Even though your plan is safe, there is no federal guarantee that every dollar you put into a 401(k) plan will be there when you're ready to take it out. If you choose investments poorly, you could lose money. Ditto if you buy and sell investments at the wrong time. And, as we all learned in the market dive of late 2008 and 2009, even if you are a careful investor, you can lose money.

Benefits from a traditional pension, or a defined benefit plan, are guaranteed by a federal agency called the Pension Benefit Guaranty Corporation (PBGC). Employers pay an annual premium rate per employee to cover the PBGC insurance. Then, if a plan is terminated, the PBGC pays a basic level of benefits to employees who were covered by the plan.

With a 401(k) plan, you are responsible for contributing to the plan and for picking good investments. The balance in your plan ultimately depends on how well you do this. It is your employer's responsibility to keep your contributions safe. And your employer is legally responsible for offering good investment choices and for supervising your money in the plan.

Those employers who elect to follow rules put in place by the Department of Labor and effective January 1, 1994, must offer at least three distinctly different choices, each of which has a different level of risk. They must also provide you with educational materials and the opportunity to move your money between the different options at least once a quarter. The rules are designed to provide you with the investment options and the tools you need to make sound choices. Capitalizing on them is your responsibility.

To do that, you should:

■ Read the material provides by your employer on plan rules and investment options.

■ Spend some time to make certain your 401(k) portfolio is diversified across different kinds of assets.

■ Do an annual "check up" to make certain you are on track.

PART THREE

HOW TO GET IN AND GET OUT

Contributing to Your 401(k) Account

You should enroll in your company's 401(k) plan. Period. But what if you're twenty-five years old and this is the first time you've had two nickels to rub together? Saving for retirement is boring. I asked a nineteen-year-old college freshman what he thinks about retirement. "Well I try not to think too much on it," he said. "But if I had to I would think about saving some money. I can't depend on anyone else to support me when I'm old." This college freshman happens to be my son, Tom. He likely would not know as much about saving and investing if his parents weren't financial journalists, yet young people today are more aware than their parents were that no one is going to support them in retirement.

But forget about retirement for a moment. Think about your life. Think about your dreams. What do you want to accomplish in your career? In your financial life? In her regular *Wall Street Journal* column, "Work & Family," Sue Shellenbarger wrote in June 2009 that our kids will need to be much more creative and adaptable in their careers than we were. "The recession is driving home a bitter truth about the 21st century job market," she wrote. "A tidy, linear path to a secure career is increasingly hard to find." So young people must learn to be entrepreneurial; they must learn to look for new opportunities.[1]

One important ingredient in reaching career goals is to put some money aside. There's no simpler way to save than by having the dollars taken out of your paycheck before you get your hands on it. And there's no better return than the 50 percent you're likely to get from your employer's match as soon as you make your first investment.

1. Sue Shellenbarger, "Raising Kids Who Can Thrive Amid Chaos in Their Careers," *Wall Street Journal*, June 10, 2009, http://online.wsj.com/article/SB124459007942099943.html.

You put in $1 and your employer adds 50 cents. Then you decide where to invest the $1.50.

Everyone knows by now that the stock market took a tumble in 2008 and 2009. The Dow Jones Industrial Average fell from its high of 14,164 in October 2007 to 6,469 in March 2009. This was not a happy time to be in the stock market. Because the crash turned so brutal, some investors believed they would be better off to leave the stock market and never get back in again. But those who fared the worst were those who exited in February and March 2009 when the market was hitting new lows day after day. Not all of them were novices. John Cammack, head of third-party distribution for T. Rowe Price, the mutual fund company based in Baltimore, confessed that despite years of advising financial advisors who work with T. Rowe and telling them to hang on through thick and thin, he got cold feet himself, selling off some stock when the market went down to 6,500. But he'd recovered his optimism by April and was back in the market all the wiser.

By mid-September, a year after the Lehman Brothers bankruptcy nearly topples the financial system, the stock market hit new highs for the year. The Dow Jones Average of 30 Industrial Stocks closed at 9683.41 on September 15, its highest lose since October 8, 2008.

Saving money while you're young is the best thing you can do for yourself. The employer match is the closest you'll ever get to found money. So get started. Even if you don't have enough information to choose investments yet, join the plan and put the money into a money market fund until you've done more research. Do not procrastinate because that is the only way you can lose money in this deal. Once you've gotten started, there are many places you can go for more information. Like you, I read the occasional book or magazine or newspaper article that says that 401(k) plans are bad for your financial health. But I know that reporters are pressured to come up with something new, and nay-saying or scare headlines brings in more readers. Certainly 401(k) plans have some negative aspects, but nothing bad enough to justify avoiding the accounts altogether.

One of the reasons many people give for failing to contribute to a 401(k) account is that the money will be locked up too long. If that's a concern for you, you'll want to know about the rules for tapping into the money when you need it. There are a number of ways to get access to your money, including 401(k) loans, which you may be able to make over the Internet. So find out how to get in and out when you need to. Then join the plan.

Where to Get Help

SO BY NOW YOU KNOW that you are expected to take responsibility for your retirement, for setting goals, and for saving money. But you don't need to start from scratch. Lots of information has been pulled together to help you in your quest for savings and security.

The human resources department is a logical place to start. Many employers hire benefit consulting firms like Hewitt Associates or Watson Wyatt or Mercer to answer participants' questions and to provide information on how to get into the plan and choose investments and so forth. Some hire mutual fund vendors to help employees sort through what they need to know. Other employers hire companies like Financial Engines, founded by Nobel Prize-winning economist William F. Sharpe, which provides online research to help participants plan for retirement and computer analytics that can help an employee look at different scenarios to determine how much money she will need to save for retirement. Other employers ask the mutual fund company that provides the investment options to handle questions about investing.

The Department of Labor issued final rules on advice-giving in January 2009, yet the topic remains controversial, with one side arguing that the advisers must be totally independent and objective, and the other saying that an adviser who represents an investment vendor can still be objective. Employees may be able to meet with someone in their company's human resources department or talk to someone over the phone or through a chat client on a Web site.

No matter the circumstances, here are the questions all participants should ask:

■ **Are workshops available?** Many companies offer financial-planning workshops for employees. Remember Ted Benna, who invented the 401(k) plan? When I spoke with him in January 2009, he was in the process of presenting six workshops for one of his client's employees, trying to answer questions about what had happened to their 401(k) accounts. Benna told them that every category of stocks was down 40 percent in 2008, and bonds got hammered too. He advised young employees to hold steady, keep pumping money in, pay off credit cards, and switch to a fixed-rate mortgage. For those closer to retirement, the question is much more difficult, he said.

■ **Is anything available on the Internet?** Some companies post 401(k) plan information online. Others use consultants to build a site that can be used by their employees.

■ **Does the company have an Intranet site with 401(k) plan information?** Many companies use their own networks to provide information to employees.

■ **How can I project retirement needs?** Most plan sponsors offer some type of modeling tool—usually a computer-based instrument—that helps employees project their account balance over time. This might be a piece of software for a personal computer or it might be an online service or part of the company's computer network. Ask your employer if there is a user's guide to lead you through it.

■ **How about simplified forms?** Financial information can be intimidating. Even the Internal Revenue Service (IRS) came up with a short form for taxes. Many employers responded to complaints about the difficulty of understanding 401(k) plan information by developing easier-to-use materials such as a one-page document of Frequently Asked Questions (FAQ).

■ **How available is the employee newsletter?** Like other employer-provided communications, your newsletter could be terrific. Or it might be a waste of time. Read an issue or two before you dismiss it.

■ **What other resources are available?** Companies take their responsibility to educate employees seriously. Many reprint and distribute articles from magazines that they feel might be helpful to employees.

The Match Makes the Magic

IF YOU'VE been reading along straight through this book, you remember that when Ted Benna designed the first 401(k) plan in 1981, what set it apart from a run-of-the-mill savings plan was that the employer offered a match to those employees who made a contribution. The match makes the magic. Without it, many employees would still contribute to get tax advantages. But surveys show that it is the match that is most important in persuading employees to sign up.

And it is the match that guarantees you a return on your money that you cannot get anywhere else. When you search for an investment that pays a good return, you will never find another that offers "free" money so that you have an immediate return as soon as you invest. The most common match is 50 percent of the employee contribution up to 6 percent of salary. The math on that is pretty simple: Say you earn $100,000 and you contribute $6,000 to your 401(k) plan, or 6 percent of your salary. Your employer kicks in another $3,000 or 50 percent of your $6,000, providing a 50 percent return on your money before you've made any investment at all. But what if you earn $60,000 and you contribute $6,000? Your match will be lower because you are contributing a larger percentage of your salary, 10 percent to be exact. Your employer matches half of the first 6 percent—or $3,600—making a contribution of $1,800.

In 2000, about 90 percent of employers provided a match and those companies that were changing their plans—and tinkering with the match—were generally increasing it to make the plan more generous. That's not the case after the stock market tsunami of 2008 though. It seemed that every day in the first half of 2009, plansponsor.com reported on more companies that dropped the employer match, oftentimes "indefinitely."

For example, at the end of March, JPMorgan Chase dropped its match for all employees and said it will reevaluate the plans later. However, employees earning $250,000 or more at JPMorgan Chase "will see their contributions discontinued indefinitely," a bank spokesman said. The move to cut the match indefinitely for employees earning more than $250,000 is an interesting one. The Obama Administration tagged earners of $250,000 and over as "the rich" and said these rich folk would pay more taxes going forward. That and the attitude of Americans that these Wall Street "rich" were to blame for our economic collapse must have made it easier for JPMorgan to make that decision.

On the Wall Street of earlier years, firms would have been reluctant to penalize "the rich" like this lest they lose them to the competition, but not any longer. A survey by Spectrem Group found that just over a third of U.S. employers cut back or cut out the match between January 2008 and February 2009. But these are the kinds of changes that spread in ripples that one day reverse themselves and head back to some more neutral position.

Employee benefits consultants, though, warned that cutting the match could be a disaster for employer/employee relationships. Bill McClain, a Mercer retirement consultant who conducted a survey on that topic said that while the loss of one year's employer contribution won't "have a huge impact" on an employee's retirement benefit, a reduction can weaken benefits already hit hard by declines in equity values. Further, it would prohibit employees from buying equities with the "match money" at historically low prices. He urged employers to try to identify cost savings that would only minimally affect employees' nest eggs.

If your employee does provide a match, don't let it slip away. Even if the match is offered only in company stock, which is not a good choice for 401(k) plan, I think you should put aside enough money to capture it.

Automatic Enrollment

REMEMBER THE RULES about discrimination testing? (see p. 69 for details.) Plan sponsors must perform tests to make certain that their plans do not unduly favor the highly paid employees over the rank and file. One important way to draw in the lower-paid employees is with the company match, of course. But in the first decade of the twenty-first century, employers and consultants began to look for a way to enroll employees in the plan so that they would automatically become participants when they joined the company unless they specifically elected to opt out.

The Pension Protection Act of 2006, the most important piece of pension legislation since ERISA, helped make automatic enrollment in 401(k) plans possible. Before that, laws in thirty-one states prohibited any paycheck deduction by an employer without employee consent. The Pension Protection Act overrode the laws in those states and allowed companies to automatically enroll an employee in the plan. But the company must tell the employees that the money will be deducted from their paychecks and deposited in the 401(k) plan, according to Kyle Brown, retirement counsel for Watson Wyatt in Washington.

The employer must also give employees the right to opt out of the plan and to get their money back after the first two paychecks if they choose, says Brown. If an employer uses automatic enrollment and follows a specific formula—deducting 3 percent of an employee's pay when he is first eligible and depositing it in the plan, increasing that to 4 percent on the employee's one-year anniversary, 5 percent on the two-year anniversary and 6 percent after three years—the employer need not perform the nondiscrimination test, Brown says. That's because all employees have been encouraged to participate.

So the provision for automatic enrollment was passed in 2006. But plan sponsors still needed guidance on which investment option was best suited for the money, or what would be the "default option" for employees who were enrolled automatically. At one time, money market funds were the default options. But the Department of Labor deemed money markets funds too conservative and stocks too aggressive, so it issued guidance on where to put this money: Under the new rules, those plans that use a balanced fund, which invests in stocks and bonds, or a target-date fund, which aims to combine a mix of investments that will provide the retirement dollars the participant needs, are permissible. So are "managed accounts," where a manager oversees the assets in the fund.

Since then, the "target date" funds have been one of the fastest growing investment options in 401(k) plans. The decision by the Department of Labor to endorse these funds as an acceptable default option for automatic enrollment ensures continued what was already robust growth in these funds. They are no longer just one choice among many. They've become the number one choice, or the default option, for most plans. By this, I don't mean to say they are the best choice but only the most popular. Part of the reason is the way they are marketed. Many investors believe they offer some sort of guarantee for those who retire in a particular year. That is not true.

The problems and disappointments with these funds became clear in 2008 when nearly all target-date funds turned in disappointing performances. Ron Surz, principal of Target Date Analytics, in San Clemente, California, performed several studies to show how these funds fell short including "The Target Date Emperor Has No Clothes," in March 2009.

Target-date funds are discussed more thoroughly in Part Four: Investing. Everyone who invests in a 401(k) plan should understand the reasoning behind these funds and how they work in practice. And they should understand that the results are in no way guaranteed. For example, even the funds with a target date of 2010 lost a good deal of money in 2008, which Surz argues is a good reason for revamping them. The people who invested in them with plans to retire a year after the crash were not in a position to withstand a 30 percent drop in their nest eggs. So you must look at these funds carefully and make a wise decision rather than simply believing they are right for you because the "target date" is the year you plan to retire.

Taking Loans

THE EASIEST WAY to tap into your 401(k) account is to take a loan from your plan. Most 401(k) plans have loan provisions. Usually, you can use the money for whatever you like—to make a down payment on a home, to buy a car, to take a vacation, or to satisfy just about any other need you have for ready cash.

Tapping your 401(k) account for a loan offers several advantages over going to a bank. First, you qualify for a loan simply by having money in the plan. Second, the interest you pay goes into your retirement account rather than to the bank. Individual employers set their own rules governing plan loans.

The Department of Labor and the Internal Revenue Service (IRS) add some requirements and rules of their own. For example, to avoid paying tax on the money, plan participants can borrow no more than 50 percent of the money in their plan. The money must be repaid within five years unless it is a loan for a home, in which case the term is set by the employer. The most common term for a 401(k) loan is ten years, but some can run up to thirty years.

Although the employer sets the interest rate, the Department of Labor prohibits loans at a below-market rate. In other words, your employer must charge you roughly the same as a bank would charge customers like you. As a result, most employers tie their interest rate to the prime rate, the base rate on corporate loans at large money-center banks.

You can expect to pay one or two percentage points above the prime. Many plans also charge loan processing and administrative fees. Bruce Bent, founder of The Reserve Primary Fund, the first money market fund, created a debit card program in 2003 that allowed 401(k) plan participants to make a loan using the card. The interest rate was set at the prime rate plus 2.9 percent.

These advantages make a 401(k) loan a good option if you are strapped for cash. Still, there are drawbacks. The biggest one is this: Most plans do not allow you to continue your repayment schedule if you leave the company. That means you must pay back the outstanding balance if you leave for whatever reason, whether you quit or are dismissed.

This became a problem for many plan participants who carried outstanding loan balances when they lost their jobs in 2009. If you do not pay back the entire balance, the remainder becomes a taxable distribution: Then you must pay tax and a 10 percent early withdrawal penalty on it that year. Imagine if you had borrowed $10,000 to do some renovation work on your home. If you lose your job and can't repay the loan you pay taxes and the 10 percent penalty by April 15, 2010.

There's also the "opportunity cost," which means your money no longer earns a market rate of return while you have it on loan.

Another snag, one pointed out by Lynn Brenner, a personal finance journalist and author of *Building Your Nest Egg with Your 401(K)*, is the hidden cost to 401(k) loans. When you borrow from your 401(k) account, you take a loan against pre-tax money, spend it, and pay it back with after-tax dollars. And then, when you retire, you pay tax a second time on those same dollars.

None of this means a 401(k) loan is out of the question. But the need for immediate cash must be great enough to offset these negatives. First, you should be certain that your job is secure. Then weigh the loan negatives against the important opportunity in your life. Should you take a 401(k) loan to fund an expensive vacation? Probably not. But perhaps you should if you are starting a business, adopting a child, or making a life-altering transition. Don't forget that you must pay the loan back before you leave your job. Compare a 401(k) loan with a home equity loan before you make a decision.

Beneficiary Designations

IT'S THE SIMPLE things that most often trip us up in financial planning. You probably don't forget to pay the mortgage. But financial planners say that clients make some of their biggest mistakes when naming beneficiaries. They suggest that a client name a spouse as beneficiary and children as contingent beneficiaries during their working years.

Once you retire and roll the money into an Individual Retirement Account (IRA), the rules become more complex. Seymour Goldberg, an attorney who specializes in retirement account issues, says he finds that clients often do not state clearly how children are to share in an IRA. For instance, a client might name his two children, John Smith and Mary Smith as beneficiaries. Under that arrangement, if John Smith dies before the account owner, Mary Smith will get half the account and the other half will be paid into the estate, Goldberg says. But usually that is not what the account owner intended. He probably wanted the money to be split between Mary Smith and John Smith, heirs, thereby treating his two children equally.

Goldberg suggests that clients who want the money shared equally between their children name the children "*issue per stirpes*," which means the children share equally. If one child dies, that child's share would go to his or her children. Goldberg says he finds that this, in fact, is what most parents intend to do and that they are surprised to learn that that will not necessarily happen if they simply name the children. If the institution that holds the account doesn't permit the *per stirpes* designation, Goldberg puts an asterisk by the name of each child with a footnote that says, "if this child dies this share goes to his or her children."

Sometimes, Goldberg says, a client, not realizing the legal implications of such an oversight, doesn't list all the intended beneficiaries simply because the form doesn't have enough lines. Even if the account owner has painstakingly listed each beneficiary properly, the custodian may eliminate some of the paperwork in the computer.

"A number of institutions can't code it properly on their computers," he says. "So even if you do it the right way and then you call the institution two years later, you find out that they destroyed your rider." This is an urgently important issue. In that case, Goldberg says, he sometimes advises the client to move the account. "We threaten them with taking the money away if they can't do it properly," he says.

Improper or missing beneficiary forms can impose punishing results on beneficiaries. For example, a surviving spouse holds special rights to an inherited IRA. Goldberg has had two cases where clients died and the brokerage firm couldn't find the form that designated the widow as beneficiary of the IRA. In the first case, the IRA contained $80,000. The widow was permitted to roll it over into her own IRA because she was the sole beneficiary of the estate and the sole executrix. Goldberg was able to cite an Internal Revenue Service (IRS) private letter ruling that permits a rollover under those circumstances.

In the other case, the widow inherited an IRA with $200,000. But here there were also some trusts involved as beneficiaries, so she was not the sole beneficiary. Because the beneficiary form was lost, the $200,000 was dumped into the estate and became immediately taxable.

Now Goldberg is advising all clients to write to their IRA custodian once every five years or so to ask for a copy of the beneficiary form. If the custodian merges with another firm, the client should write to the merged firm to make certain that the beneficiary form survived the merger. If it's lost, it's a simple matter to provide a new one, as long as the client makes certain to do it before the IRA owner dies.

If the Plan Fails the Test

WE'VE ALREADY DISCUSSED the fact that Federal laws dictate that 401(k) plans cannot discriminate unfairly in favor of high-income employees. If the plan includes an automatic enrollment provision (see p. 94), it need not be tested because everyone gets a good shot at participating.

If it does not, it must be tested. Suppose the test finds the plan to be discriminatory. What then? It can be disqualified, which means it loses its tax benefits. To prove that a plan does not discriminate, the sponsor must complete a series of tests referred to as annual deferral percentage (ADP) tests. This means looking at the contribution made by the higher-paid group as a whole and the lower-paid group as a whole and comparing them to make certain that the higher paids are not getting more than their share of benefit.

Under the old rules, the plan was required to pass the discrimination test 12 months after the close of the plan year, which is generally December 31. To satisfy the requirement the plan sponsor typically tested the plan early in the year. If it failed the test, the sponsor was required to return to certain highly compensated employees their contributions, which were taxable.

The 2006 Pension Protection Act modified this rule so that employers could satisfy the nondiscrimination rules by using figures from the year-earlier date. This was an improvement both for sponsors and participants because it makes it far less likely that employees will get taxable contributions handed back to them.

In order to conduct the nondiscrimination test, the plan administrator splits the employees into two groups: those who are highly compensated and those who are not. The Small Business Job Protection Act of 1996 raised the dividing line between the two groups from $66,000 to $80,000. Those who made $80,000 or more were considered highly compensated and those who earned $79,999 were not considered highly compensated.

That figure increased gradually until it reached $110,000 for 2009. The administrator determines how much the lower-paid group contributes to the plan on average. Let's suppose it's 2 percent. That means the highly compensated group can contribute no more than 4 percent on average, because the spread between the contributions of the two groups generally cannot exceed 2 percentage points.

Traditionally, or at least until the market crash in 2008, plan sponsors worked hard to get the lower paid employees to contribute so that the higher paid employees could contribute more. Tax deferral—and other tax benefits—are generally worth more to highly paid workers because they are in a higher tax bracket. Of course, they also have more discretionary income whereas lower paid workers are typically spending a larger percent of income on necessities.

I think the 2008 market crash has altered this ratio a bit. That's chiefly because the gulf between the highly paid workers—those who many Americans now see as the culprits in the financial mess—and the lower paid workers has become so much more visible. And it's clear which side the good guys are on. President Obama and his agenda have a good deal to do with that.

A year after the crash, less mention is being made of the lower paid workers—some of whom stretched too far to take out a mortgage—than the higher paid workers who are being blamed for the mortgage crisis due to the highly leveraged instruments they created.

Banks, in particular, were taken to task with the *New York Times* reporting on September 24, 2009 that Adair Turner, Britain's top financial regulator, "is daring to ask the very question that many Britons, and indeed, many Americans, are asking themselves: What good are banks if all they do is push money?"

Perhaps that's why, when JPMorgan Chase announced that it was dropping the match for its 401(k) plan, it added that although the match would be back for most workers, it was suspended permanently for those employees earning more than $250,000.

After-Tax Contributions

MANY 401(k) PLANS permit after-tax contributions. Although these contributions are clearly not as appealing as putting in money before it's taxed, some employees should still consider it.

If you're not contributing as much as you can to your plan already, this is not for you. Your first goal should be to max out on your pre-tax 401(k) plan contribution. For many people, that means $16,500 if you are forty-nine or younger and $22,000 for those fifty and older.

But some employees—those whom the government considers highly compensated—are usually not permitted to contribute up the dollar limit. Instead, their limit is determined by the relationship between higher-paid and lower-paid contributors. The plan might limit them to a certain percent of salary—say 5 percent—based on what percentage of pay is contributed by lower-paid workers.

Some of these employees may qualify to make pre-tax contributions to a supplemental, non-qualified plan (see p. 76) But for many of them, the only choice will be to make after-tax contributions.

How to decide? You might compare an after-tax 401(k) contribution to buying an annuity contract or contributing to a nondeductible Individual Retirement Account (IRA). All three of these investments are made with after-tax dollars. But earnings accumulate tax free until the money is withdrawn. The after-tax 401(k) plan provides a couple of advantages over the other two, though.

The major disadvantage to a nondeductible IRA is that accounting can be a nightmare. You are responsible for keeping track of which money has been taxed, which has not, and the earnings on each. In a 401(k) plan, the plan administrator takes care of this headache.

The downside of an annuity contract (which is an investment purchased from an insurance company) is that it includes some underwriting, or insurance, costs that you must pay. The costs cut into your investment earnings. An after-tax 401(k) plan does not have these problems.

The after-tax money is generally easier to tap into than the pre-tax savings, as well. For example, when Ed Emerman founded his own public relations firm, Eagle, in Princeton, New Jersey, his former employer cut him a separate check for his after-tax savings. That money came in handy for a business start-up. (After-tax money is not eligible for rollover to an IRA.)

Many companies also allow you to tap into the money even while you're still on the job, according to Ethan Kra, chief actuary at Mercer, New York-based management consultants. However, when you withdraw after-tax money that you contributed after January 1987, the Internal Revenue Service (IRS) considers a portion of it to be taxable earnings, which are also subject to the 10 percent early withdrawal penalty if you are younger than age 59½. Say you've contributed $10,000 after tax, and it has earned $1,000. Of every dollar you withdraw, 10 cents will be taxable in addition to the 10 percent withdrawal penalty. Unlike the Roth 401(k), which allows you to withdraw principal first, this after-tax 401(k) account splits each dollar you withdraw into "taxable" and "already taxed."

Some employers have supplemental executive retirement plans (or SERPs) that allow employees to contribute pre-tax dollars to an unsecured plan. But these plans are typically only available for the company's top executives or highly compensated employees, a definition that depends on "facts and circumstances," rather than just the amount of compensation, according to Kyle Brown, retirement counsel for Wyatt Watson. So those employees who earn more than the $110,000 limit in 2009 (a number that will be indexed for inflation), and too little to qualify for the supplemental plan, are prime candidates to tuck away some savings in after-tax contributions.

Supplemental Plans

OVER THE PAST SEVERAL YEARS, employers have been scrambling to set up supplemental pension plans for employees because of the growing limits on regular pension plans that we have been discussing. Even those employees happy to be covered in the new plans, though, might get unpleasant surprises at retirement. The supplemental plans do not offer the same security or tax advantages as traditional plans.

Regular pension plans, including both defined benefit plans and 401(k) plans, are called "qualified plans" because they meet certain rules and receive special tax treatment. The company, or plan sponsor, gets a deduction for any contribution it makes and employees do not pay any tax until they receive the benefit. Even when they retire, employees can roll the money over into an Individual Retirement Account (IRA) and continue to defer taxes. As discussed earlier, the government tries to maintain a delicate balance between encouraging Americans to save for their own retirement and preserving tax revenue.

Over the years, qualified plans have been cut back for upper-income employees to help bolster tax revenue. Recruiting top people for corporate and Wall Street jobs has been a tough business. Many companies try to make up for lost benefits by setting up supplemental executive retirement plans, called SERPs, which are non-qualified plans. SERPS represent a portion of the promised retirement benefit for many employees, but that is not portion guaranteed.

Most employees think of retirement benefits as one piece. They do not understand part of the benefits may come from a secured, qualified plan and another portion from an unfunded, non-qualified plan. "Many people would be shocked to see that the overwhelming portion of their pension is coming from a SERP and only a small amount from the qualified plan," one consultant told me.

There are two serious drawbacks to the SERPs. Supplemental plans are merely a promise to pay a benefit; the money for these benefits is not set aside with your name on it or secured in any way. So the employee faces the risk that the employer cannot pay or that it reneges on the contract. These plans also lack tax advantages. When a retiree gets this money, a chunk off the top goes for taxes. The remainder cannot be shielded in a tax-deferred retirement account, meaning future earnings are taxed as well.

I haven't seen any news yet on how SERPs might be affected by the new "frugality" on Wall Street. I put it in quotes because I'm not sure that Wall Street can ever be frugal.

But the spotlight is focused on big finance in the fall of 2009, particularly on the banks. I see that because, beginning in the spring of 2009, I have been functioning as news editor of a new web site for financial advisors, advisorsforadvisors.com. Every morning, beginning at 4:30 a.m., I go online to read the *Financial Times,* the *New York Times,* the *Wall Street Journal,* Reuters, Bloomberg, *USA Today, Real Clear Markets,* and so forth, and post what I consider to be the most important stories to that site.

So it was that I watched the "green shoots" of spring sprouting in the global economy, followed by the pickup in world markets. But by the end of September, plenty of questions were being raised about the strength of the recovery, in particular regarding the role of banks.

On September 25, Reuters reported that "the level of losses from syndicated loans facing banks and other financial institutions tripled to $53 billion in 2009, due to poor underwriting standards and the continuing weakness in economic conditions."[2]

And a story in the *New York Times* on September 23 reported that Britain's chief financial regulator, Adair Turner, refused to let the banks off the hook for their role in the crisis even though his critics called him "crackers," and "stupid."[3]

The *Times* reported that "Mr. Turner is daring to ask the very question that many Britons, and indeed, many Americans, are asking themselves: What good are banks if all they do is push money around and enrich themselves?"

I think Mr. Turner is on to something and I expect we'll see more pressure on the financial institutions to prove their worth. Won't some of that focus on the inequality in retirement benefits, such as SERPS, being provided to the "higher paids," vs. the "lower paids," many of whom are out of work?

---

2. Reuters, Reuters./com, http://www.reuters.com/article/ousivMolt/idUSTRE58O1HR 20090925.

3. *New York Times,* nytimes.com, http://www.nytimes.com/2009/09/24/business/global/ 24turner.html?_r=1&hp.

Getting Out Early

YOU KNOW by now that there is a 10 percent penalty levied on retirement money that is withdrawn before you reach age 59½. But there are some exceptions to that rule. Perhaps the most significant one allows employees who leave their companies at age 55 or older to take the money in corporate retirement plans without paying the penalty.

"If you actually worked on your fifty-fifth birthday, and you separated from service one day later, you can take the money," says Ethan E. Kra, chief actuary for retirement at Mercer in New York. "You could be fired, you could quit, or you could just walk out the door and not tell them where you're going. The reason is immaterial."

That may be a comfort for people in their fifties who consider their jobs tenuous. Taking another job does not disqualify you for the penalty-free withdrawal. The right to take the money at age fifty-five is independent of anything else you do.

This early payout, however, applies only to tax-qualified retirement plans like 401(k) plans, not to IRAs. Nor is it available to employees who quit working or retire before age fifty-five.

Suppose you work for a company where you qualify for early retirement after thirty years of service. Maybe you've completed the thirty years at age fifty-two. But if you quit then, your money will be locked up until age 59½. In other words, qualifying for early retirement from the company does not entitle you to use the exemption.

Of course, any money withdrawn from tax-deferred accounts is subject to income tax. You could minimize the tax bite by taking just a chunk of the money, enough to live on until age 59½.

The other option for getting at retirement money without paying a penalty is what the Internal Revenue Service (IRS) calls "annuitizing," or taking substantially equal payments based on life expectancy. The annuitizing method can be used for IRAs as well as for qualified plans and can be used at any age.

To qualify, a participant must take substantially equal payments for five years or until age 59½, whichever comes later. The IRS permits three different methods for annuitizing. With the first, calculations are based solely on life expectancy. The second includes a reasonable interest rate on the money as well as life expectancy. The third allows the use of an annuity table.

The first produces the smallest annual payout; the third, the largest, but the difference is only a few hundred dollars on a lump sum of $100,000 for a fifty-year-old.

The older you are and the more money you have, the better the annuitizing method looks. A forty-seven-year-old has a life expectancy of 35.9 years. Annuitizing a $100,000 balance by the simplest method would amount to annual payments of just $2,800. Certainly you couldn't expect to support yourself on that! And you would be required to pay tax on it.

But look how a few years and a few hundred thousand dollars changes the picture. A fifty-two-year-old who begins annuitizing a $750,000 balance that is expected to grow at 6 percent a year could take out $50,624 a year until age eighty-two, according to Kra. Leaving the money untouched is always your best option, but you should know what your other options are.

Another important point to consider here is that you must think of how you will support yourself well beyond the age of 82. As I've reported elsewhere, longevity risk is the biggest risk we face in retirement (see p. 214).

Kra has done considerable work on longevity risk. He would surely advise us not to plan to run out of money at age 82, as in the example above. Indeed, it is in the years after your 85th birthday that you will be least likely to be able to work and will most need to receive an income. As noted on p. 214, Kra believes the best option for those later years is longevity insurance.

10

Changing Jobs

IF YOU'RE NOT CAREFUL, a couple of things might trip up your 401(k) plan during a job change. First, you must repay any outstanding loan on your plan when you leave your job. If you do not, the money is treated as a distribution and becomes taxable.

Second, you must take care to be certain that the entire account does not become taxable. In 1992, Congress imposed a 20 percent withholding tax on lump-sum retirement distributions that are paid directly to employees who change jobs, retire, or are laid off.

The law, effective January 1, 1993, provides that employees who take their retirement money in a lump sum when they leave their job will receive only 80 percent, with the other 20 percent withheld for tax. Prior to 1993, 401(k) plan participants could take a check for the entire amount and defer all taxes if they rolled it over within sixty days to an Individual Retirement Account (IRA).

Here's what to do to avoid the tax:

■ Have your employer roll the money directly into an IRA. If you decide to do this, set up a separate IRA called a conduit IRA to receive the money. Doing so preserves your right to roll the money into another employer's plan later. Such a rollover might be attractive because IRA money is not eligible for certain favorable tax treatments nor can it be borrowed. Both are possible with money in employer-sponsored plans.

■ Leave the money in your employer's plan. This will preserve your options.

■ Begin making periodic withdrawals from the plan based on your life expectancy. This option, called annuitizing, is available no matter what your age. (see p. 106) You must pay tax on the money as you receive it but you avoid a 10 percent penalty on premature withdrawals otherwise assessed if you are younger than 59½. If you choose to annuitize, you must continue making the withdrawals for five years or until you are 59½, whichever is later.

■ Transfer the money directly to your new employer's plan. Transferring the money may not be an option as some plans impose a one-year waiting period before you are allowed to join.

Many people who lose their jobs worry that they will need the money from their retirement plans to live on and feel reluctant to have an employer make a direct transfer to an IRA. The law provides that if you take the money in a check—less the 20 percent—you can still roll it over to an IRA and receive a full refund of the withheld portion when you file tax returns for the year.

But that is true only if the total amount, including what was withheld, is deposited. Suppose you receive $40,000 from a $50,000 distribution, with the other $10,000 withheld for tax. You could get a refund of that $10,000, but only if you added $10,000 of your own money to the $40,000 you received from your employer and put that total amount into an IRA within sixty days of the distribution.

If instead you roll over just the $40,000, you get only a partial refund. You will be taxed on the $10,000 and assessed a 10 percent penalty for early withdrawal ($1,000) if you are younger than 59½. State taxes may also be due. By the time you discover this conundrum, it may be too late. "People who are less sophisticated about rollovers will take the check and discover too late that they can't raise the money," says Kra.

If you lose your job and feel uncertain about what to do, ask your employer to roll over the money into an IRA. If you find later that you don't have enough money to live on, you can withdraw a chunk of it—even the very next day—and you are no further behind. "You should always keep all your options open," says Glenn S. Daily, a fee-only insurance consultant in New York.

Increasingly, keeping your options open requires that you be familiar with these sometimes arcane rules. Don't count on a friend—or even your employer—to interpret them. Do your own research.

Coordinating with Your Spouse

WE FREQUENTLY HEAR that money issues drive more couples apart than anything else besides sex. So now that you have a retirement plan, experts suggest that you coordinate your investment choices with those of your spouse so that you can make the most out of your 401(k) plans. Yikes! Deciding how to manage retirement benefits and allocate both dollars and investment options between spouses is a complex issue—one that could keep a team of psychologists busy.

But it is important for couples to face this issue. Legally, a pension—which includes 401(k) plans—belongs only to the participant in the plan. There are some loaded issues here. Coordinating your benefits makes some assumption about the longevity of your relationship. Each spouse must feel that he or she is getting a fair shake in retirement dollars. That means putting aside money in each spouse's name even though it may not be possible to put the same amount aside for each spouse because of different types of retirement plans and different levels of compensation.

While you should aim for equity in the retirement dollars you put aside for each spouse, you should also try to squeeze the most you can from the two plans. Although couples seem to be increasingly adept at making the most of their health insurance plans by picking the best from each spouse's coverage, I'm not sure the same strategy has been applied to 401(k) plans.

Here are some issues to consider:

■ **Matching.** If you cannot afford to fully fund both spouses' 401(k) plans, be certain to at least capture the employer match in each one.

■ **Vesting.** Pay attention to vesting, which refers to the time it takes before you actually own the employer match. If you leave before you are vested, you leave the match behind.

■ **Investments.** Here you as a couple have the opportunity to do some real coordination. Probably each spouse's plan provides limited choices. You may as well make the best of what each plan has to offer, provided, of course, that you see eye to eye on investments.

An investment portfolio should include a large-company stock fund or an index fund or exchange-traded fund as the core. If one of the two plans offers an index fund like the Vanguard Index 500 Trust or Standard & Poor's Index of 500 Stocks (SPY), an electronically traded fund that invests in the Standard & Poor's 500 Index, go for it. You should also consider a small-company fund, an international fund and perhaps some exposure to emerging markets. It makes good sense to pick the best of the funds from each plan to build a retirement portfolio without overlaps. Still, I think it's critical that each spouse feel good about the elections in his or her own plan. So if the husband has a great emerging-market fund, but he just can't stomach that kind of volatility, I suggest he pass it by.

A retirement plan is often a couple's biggest asset outside the home. If the couple divorces, the pension goes to the one who owns it. It can be split between the two partners only if the court issues a domestic relations order and the administrator of the plan "qualifies" the order, or makes certain that it meets the plan's requirements. This qualified domestic relations order, or QDRO, splits the retirement plan according to the couple's agreement.

QDROs were authorized by the Retirement Equity Act of 1984, which addressed spousal rights to a pension. The act became effective January 1, 1985. Before that date, it was possible to split pension assets in divorce, but a court order was directed at the spouse with the pension, rather than at the pension plan itself. For example, the husband might be told by the court that once he began to receive a monthly pension, perhaps fifteen years in the future, he should send half to his former wife. But if he died before retirement, the wife would have received nothing under the old rules.

PART FOUR

INVESTING

Saving for Retirement

For many Americans, a 401(k) plan is the first brush with the investment world. More than 68 percent of households that purchased their first mutual fund in 2000 or later bought that fund through an employer-sponsored plan, according to the Investment Company Institute, the trade group for mutual funds. How can you make choices about investments that will play such a large role in determining your financial future?

The American worker used to retire with a pension, a social security check, personal savings, and the equity in his home. Today, everyone must invest. You must invest if you are to reach for your dreams, if you are to have the life you want. With a 401(k) plan, you can start small, make regular systematic investments and get lots of information from your employer about the investment options in your plan.

Successful investing requires a plan and a strategy. Your initial plan might be just to tuck the money away in a guaranteed investment in your plan. Learn about the basics. Be disciplined. When you develop your plan, stick with it through thick and thin. Don't get sidetracked by the "hot funds" or the "hot stocks."

But what about the market crash of 2008? Total U.S. retirement market assets, including both defined contribution and defined benefit plans, tumbled 24 percent to $7.86 trillion in 2008, down from $10.3 trillion the previous year, according to a report by Spectrem Group, a research and consulting firm based in Chicago. In a follow-up study in March 2009, Spectrem reported that 34 percent of companies had reduced or eliminated matching funds to employee 401(k) plans, and 29 percent planned to do so in the next twelve months. The survey also found that 20 percent of employees had decreased the amount they were saving in their plans and another 5 percent said they would probably do so in the next twelve months.

What I Did

I'VE ALWAYS considered myself a big risk taker. When I was a kid, I jumped out of second-story windows and drove in stock-car races. In 1996, we bought a home in the country, even though we hadn't yet closed on our apartment in New York. Our family of four lived in a rented cabin with no heat for six weeks while I went on a book tour. Give me a risk and I'll take it. Some people call it thrill seeking.

When the stock market headed higher, higher, higher, in 1987, I had to get in on it, right? But I'd never bought stock before. What should I choose? I attended a press luncheon at Drexel Burnham Lambert (remember the junk-bond king?), and an analyst told us there was plenty of room for more growth in American Express. I bought it—right before the market crash in October 1987.

How many mistakes can we count there?

1. I invested for emotional reasons, afraid that I might lose out on getting rich, like everyone else.

2. I didn't know anything about specific companies, but I thought buying an individual stock was more daring, and more rewarding, than buying a mutual fund.

3. I bought on a "tip."

4. Perhaps worst of all, after the crash, I refused to sell American Express until it got back to what I paid for it. This is a timid saver mentality, not an investor mentality. As an investor, you should look at what the stock is worth and whether you believe it will get there. I didn't know how to do that.

By the late 1990s, I was writing a weekly online investment column for MSN Money, and I knew quite a bit more about investing. I bought the hot tech stocks and doubled my money. In early 2000, I thought the market was toppy, and I sold off the tech stuff. This was my best call. On March 10, 2000, the Nasdaq hit its high of 5,048 and then tumbled to just over 1,100 on October 9, 2002. I was mostly in cash. But I congratulated myself far too much for having some secret sixth sense that steered me in the right direction.

So now we move ahead to 2008. I have my son Tom's college account invested aggressively in health care and international. My own account is a bit more conservative with some value funds like Dodge & Cox Stock and Longleaf Partners, both of which I've held for a long time. Both took a terrible drubbing in 2008 and 2009.

When the market began to retreat in September 2008 and then to go into free fall in October, I felt concerned about Tom's college account. But I'd finally learned my lesson, finally discovered that buy and hold was the way to go.

Yes, I was buy and hold. I am self-employed, so I have an IRA rather than the 401(k) plan that many employees have. I'd last looked at the account, which I keep at Charles Schwab, when it contained around $450,000. The best way for me to discipline myself is not to look, and I decided not to look again until the market stopped falling and started climbing. But here I am writing another book on 401(k) plans and investing, and I can't even face my own losses in the worst bear market we've seen in seventy years? That's bad.

So, on the morning of March 6, 2009, the day after the market dropped another 300 points to 6,594.44, I called up my online account at Charles Schwab.

The result? My account balance was $245,335. I'd lost $50,500 in what I consider my "core holding," the Standard & Poor's Index of 500 Stocks (SPY), which trades as an exchange-traded fund (ETF). I've used SPY as a portfolio core because it represents the overall market. I figure if the market goes up, SPY will ride along with it. Same goes for down. I'd started buying SPY in 1998 when it traded at $98 a share, buying in when it dipped. Now I saw that the fifty-two-week range was 68.17 to 144.30. So I bought 100 shares of SPY at 68.80.

Did I do the right thing? I don't know. I guess I did the hopeful thing, showing my belief that the entire world economy would not collapse, that all the stocks in the S&P 500 would not be reduced to 0. Most important though, I think I did a rational thing. I didn't jump on or off the bandwagon. I didn't sell off all my stocks. I didn't throw what cash I had left into the market. I bought what I thought was the most solid investment in a time of market crisis.

Expert One

YOU PROBABLY want to know what the experts did. To find out, I called Don Phillips, whom I've known professionally since 1986, not long after he rolled out of graduate school and into a job of founding Morningstar Mutual Funds, a company that revolutionized the fund industry. Some claim Morningstar's rating system of giving each fund a star rating of one to five—five being highest—was the key to opening fund investing to the rest of us.

Morningstar revolutionized mutual funds because Phillips and his colleagues began telling us the truth about funds. Before Morningstar's ratings, we had marketing materials from the fund companies and information from the Investment Company Institute, the industry trade group, and from data services that were paid by the mutual funds themselves. If I was working on a story and thought I had the dirt on some mutual fund, I could trust Phillips to confirm or tell me I was off-base. Never did I think he told me that because of some secret agenda.

"The basics of financial planning have not changed," Phillips says. He says that if you go to a financial planner at any time in your career, you will get this two-part advice: Save and invest. When you start out in your career, you should build up a nest egg that would last you for six months. At the time of retirement, you should have savings (or cash equivalents) to last three to five years. Phillips says that people talk about how terrible the market is, how they plan to retire this year but they've lost 40 percent of the 401(k) money that they'd counted on for retirement. "If you have five years of cash, you don't have to worry about how terrible the market is," he says. And he's right. When we blame the investment banks and the insurers and all the other companies for leveraging too much, we ought to take a look in our own backyard. Were you carrying too much debt when the market plunged? I was. Had you stretched to the limit to take out a super-big mortgage? Did you have money set aside in cash for near-term needs? I didn't. I lost 50 percent of my son's college account just as he was about to start college.

Phillips admires John Templeton, who built a successful mutual fund company by sticking with a prudent investment strategy. Templeton paid cash for automobiles. He paid cash for a house. "The mutual fund industry never talked about saving because that's not what it gets paid for," Phillips says. That's the part we need to do on our own. Templeton donated 10 percent of his income to the church, and he still managed to build his own wealth and that of his investors. "That kind of discipline, learning to live within your means, is out of fashion," Phillips says.

"The problem is that people expect to live like their parents when they graduate from college," Phillips says. "My wife and I lived in the cheapest part of town. We didn't have a car. We saved regularly. And we said: 'This is what we're going to do.'" They rented cheap apartments because they didn't see any value in paying high rent. They now live in Lincoln Park, a lovely part of Chicago. Phillips says many recent college graduates live in his neighborhood, paying $2,000 a month in rent.

Phillips and his wife got out of college at the University of Texas with no debt, thanks partly to low-cost tuition. Texas charged Phillips $4 a semester hour because he was a resident; Anne paid $40 because she was an out-of-state resident. They got married in 1985. Anne worked at the Federal Reserve Bank until 2000 when they had their third child and first daughter. And they continue to follow the same basic financial planning rules even though Phillips became a multimillionaire when Morningstar went public in May 2005.

"It really bothers me when people say that everything we learned is a lie," Phillips says. "They say it is somehow nefarious and it's a scam and you were all cheated. That's the most dangerous thing out there: all that cynicism." Investing is hard, Phillips says. There have been numerous really tough periods like the end of 2008 and beginning of 2009. But people have counted on the investment and real estate markets to do the heavy lifting, and they just spent whatever they wanted.

If we get one lesson from this time of market doldrums, I hope it is that we each must take responsibility for ourselves and teach our kids to do the same.

Expert Two

I ALSO CALLED ROSS LEVIN, president of Accredited Investors, a wealth management firm in Minneapolis. I haven't known Ross for quite as long as Don Phillips, but for almost as long.

At the time I got to know Don Phillips, I'd started writing columns and books and giving speeches to financial advisors. Before that, I'd been writing about the mutual fund industry from the consumer's perspective for some years, trying to make advice accessible to readers of *Woman's Day, Family Circle, McCall's,* and *Ladies Home Journal* and writing articles for *Reader's Digest* and *USA Today.* In 1986, Bob Veres, whom many in the financial planning industry see as a guru and, of course, others dislike, was editor of *Financial Planning* magazine. He asked me to write a mutual fund column, and I've been writing columns for financial planning magazines ever since. This was a time of huge change in the financial planning industry, where those planners who were independent, who served as fiduciaries for their clients rather than as salesmen pocketing a commission, made an indelible mark on the profession, and continue to do so.

Ross Levin is one of a small group of planners who came together in 1992, called themselves the Alpha Group, and began sharing information and goals and standards. Levin is also a person of honesty and integrity who tells a straight story. When I talked with him in March 2009, Levin told me that his firm hadn't lost any clients in 2008 but that the assets he managed for clients (assets under management or AUM) had declined from around $740 million to $500 million. "I've never seen investor psychology like this," Levin said. "My clients think the market will go to zero." Levin writes a column for the *Minneapolis Star Tribune,* in which he's told people that when things are too bad to be true, they're not true. "I don't think it's as bad as people think," he said. But he acknowledged that investor psychology drives the market, and with people expecting the market to go to zero, things weren't looking good.

The 2008 market represented the worst time in his career of managing money, Levin said, because all the asset classes blew up at the same time. That happened in 1987 when the Japanese market blew up, Levin said, but then the markets bounced back quickly. In the technology crash of 2000, the Standard & Poor's Index of 500 stocks was down 50 percent and the Nasdaq was down 80 percent. Levin's clients lost 11 percent that year. But in 2008, when the market was down 50 percent, Levin's clients lost 35 percent.

I asked Levin if he was making any changes in his recommendations to clients with 401(k) plans. His firm does not charge clients for advice about 401(k) plans. The only change the firm made was to increase the amount of cash clients held. At the end of 2007, he raised at least three years worth of cash in 401(k) portfolios. "For our clients close to retirement, we're going to get cash by putting new contributions into a money market fund," he said.

As for other investments, "We are fundamental believers in mean reversion," Levin said, meaning that market prices will revert toward the mean or average. But he knows from studying behavioral finance that losses mean twice as much as gains to investors. In other words, an investor who loses $50 is much more distressed than an investor who gains $50 is happy. Investors love to make money, but they hate losing it even more. Good financial advisors like Levin know that. Levin had three clients—one with $4.5 million, one with $3.5 million, and one with $2 million—who took everything out of stocks in early March when the market was at a twelve-year low. They locked in their losses. Within a week, all three wanted to get back into the market.

Levin and his team have not lost their faith in asset allocation. But the volatile markets of 2008 and 2009 caused them to move from passive investing to active investing. Passive investors simply allocate investments across broad market indexes and leave them be (see p. 142). Active investors attempt to do better than the indexes by underweighting and overweighting certain sectors of the market in addition to trading. For example, when Levin's firm was up over 100 percent on its investment in New Asia within a couple of months, they sold it off. In a bull market, it's tough to beat the indexes, Levin says, when everything is going up. But in a bear market, active managers may be able to identify stocks that will go against the trend.

Expert Three

I DIDN'T CALL ROBERT MARKMAN to get his advice on investing because I know what his advice has been in the past. I include him in this section only to show that you must have discipline and stick with your plan regardless of what you read in the newspaper or see on the Internet. *Never* buy or sell investments based on something you read or hear on television. Indeed, you should look for contrary indicators, and I think Bob Markman may be one of them.

Markman is a financial advisor and mutual fund entrepreneur based in Minneapolis. Before I criticize his first dramatic move—advising clients in the spring of 1999 to put all their money in growth stocks and growth mutual funds—I must say that his advice looked mighty tempting at the time. Until the late 1990s, I had considered myself a value investor or an investor in stocks and stock mutual funds that searched for hidden value in companies. When I talked with Henry Emerson, editor of the *Outstanding Investor Digest: Perspectives and Activities of the Nation's Most Successful Money Managers*—a newsletter that has achieved something of a cult status among the value cognoscenti—I felt that I was in the presence of genius and that the value investors he wrote about, like Warren Buffett, were the smartest investors, those who bought when investments were out of favor and made hay. But in the final years of the twentieth century, the value funds in my portfolio were shrinking while the tech stocks were doubling and tripling and more. It seemed like the end of the old era and the beginning of something new.

Markman certainly thought so. He claimed that asset allocation was dead. The only asset category he found worth investing in was large cap growth. He told me that he'd identified the five strongest mutual funds in America: Janus 20, White Oak Growth, Rydex OTC, Marsico Focus, and Papp America Abroad. "If these are the best funds I can find, why should I invest in worse funds?" he asked. I thought he was a bit reckless. In truth mutual funds perform well in different environment. No one fund is always on top. In 2000, Markman came out with a book, *Hazardous to Your Wealth: Extraordinary Popular Delusions and the Madness of Mutual Fund Experts*, in which he argued that diversification among different types of stocks—an article of faith among investment experts—only dilutes investment profits. Instead, Markman said, stocks of large, fast-growing companies, primarily the tech giants, should dominate your portfolio. The book was published with very bad timing. The tech bubble burst at about the time it come out. *Kiplinger's* magazine inducted Markman into its Mutual Hall of Shame in 2003, commenting that "investors in Markman's four funds lost their shirts," when the tech bubble burst.

But guess what happened in the first quarter of 2009? Markman pronounced that stocks are no place for the individual investors. "Americans are now taking far too much risk in their portfolios," he said. Worse yet, he wrote a column in the *Minneapolis Star Tribune* accusing financial advisors who told their clients to buy and hold during the market crash of using a "Rambo strategy" and of working against the best interest of their clients. A decade after Markman had claimed that growth stocks were the only way to go for the smart investor, he opined that we little guys should not be investing in stocks at all, and we wouldn't be if left to our own devices. He went on to blame this disaster on financial planners who sold stocks to clients only so that they could earn more commissions.

Yes, we certainly do respect free speech. But the danger of an adviser like Markman is that he might convince investors to forsake their strategy at the worst time, locking in their losses. Don't do that. Whenever people start saying: This time is different, this is a new era, the old rules don't apply, sit down and mull it over carefully. Don't bail on your plan because of something scary you read in the newspaper or see online. Remember what an investor like Don Phillips of Morningstar says: Be prudent. Pay off debt. Save and invest.

Behavioral Finance

WHY HAS INVESTING grown so complicated? The world is more complicated, of course, but another problem is that economic and investment theories that were viewed as forever workable twenty years ago have been turned on their heads by new experiments.

Consider the efficient market theory. Efficient market theory holds that all information about securities is known and is reflected in the stock prices, and so every security is rationally and appropriately priced. There is so much knowledge available, this theory holds, and so many knowledgeable players in the market that any changes in stock prices are due to random forces, almost mechanical forces, and market prices will quickly reset to again reflect, appropriately, the value of the security. Of course, anyone who has ever invested in a stock knows that this theory is pure folly. If it were true, little money would ever be made in the stock market.

In the 1980s, a group of economists began talking about what they called "behavioral economics" or "behavioral finance." They argued that people do not always choose an investment rationally. Imagine that! Indeed, these economists said, they detected all kinds of situations in which psychology had more influence on a decision than did economic reality. For example, investors hate to lose much more than they enjoy winning. They feel much more upset by a near miss than by an event they missed by a mile. Behavioral Economists like Meir Statman at Santa Clara University study the way investors make decisions and how cognition errors and emotions affect these decisions. For instance, investors show overconfidence, believing they have more control over life circumstances than they, in fact, do.

Initially these new theories—the ones that argued that cognitive bias can influence asset prices—were controversial. Economists in these new fields, like Richard Thaler at the University of Chicago, an early researcher in behavioral finance, were viewed with suspicion. Surely they'd made mistakes in their experiments if they found that man could be irrational. This was not the economic model! This was not the truth!

Behavioral economists found dozens of ways that investors, and consumers, make financial decisions based on something other than rationality. For example, entrepreneurs tend to be overconfident investors, investing in the things they know and understand rather than diversifying. Likewise, people invest too much in local companies and way too much in the stock of the company they work for because they trust what they know even though they shouldn't, as the employees at and investors in Enron found out when that company, once one of the biggest in the world, collapsed and filed for bankruptcy in December 2001.

Behaviorists also tell us that people are much more influenced by their own recent experiences than by some long-range average or "norm." So it is that investors in 2000 believed the stock market was headed up and up and up and their only task was to get their money on the table. Likewise, in 2009, investors were shell-shocked. They believed that the markets would go to zero, that every single penny they had invested would disappear.

We can sum up behavioral finance by saying that it explains all the various ways that people save, spend, and invest their money—ways that an economist of twenty years ago would call irrational. We certainly don't have to go so far as gambling to find examples of that. So a behaviorist would say that markets are often inefficient, yet the inefficiencies are not so clear as to provide wealth building opportunities. Indeed, the only rule that is tried and true is that if everyone is running toward you, you should run the other way. Do not follow the herd. The market rebound from March 2009 to September 2009 once again showed that despair, which was everywhere in March, turned quickly and starting with a few contrarian investors, built to a major rally before many investors recognized the pace of recovery.

Taking Risks

THE FIRST PIECE OF ADVICE a financial planner usually gives to a client is to get a notion of how much risk he can tolerate. Until recently, most Americans saw risk as a rollercoaster, the economy and stock market had their ups and downs but always came through in the end.

A decade ago, none of us could imagine that, even if we chose investments wisely, we might lose 35 percent of our money, or even 50 percent of our money, as some investors did in 2008 and 2009.

Then came the housing bubble, the housing bust, and the market collapse of 2008 and 2009. This time seemed different with financial institutions that were household names like Citibank and Bank of America begging for government money while the automakers headed toward bankruptcy and unemployment soared.

Of course, investing is risky. So is not investing. If you think that risk simply means that you might lose the dollar you have in your hand, you need to broaden your thinking. If you are too conservative, you risk losing new opportunities, losing your chance for a better life.

The most basic risk investors face is not an academic one but an emotional one: The fear that the money they invest will decline in value, even temporarily. A decline in the value of an investment makes many people feel both foolish and anxious. When these people think about risk, it means one simple thing: What is the risk to my principal? If I invest $10,000, is there any chance that my money will ever be worth less than $10,000? Can some of it disappear in a mysterious way? Could it be worth just $9,500 the day after I invest it?

For those who look at risk in this way, the choices are bank certificates of deposit and Treasury bills. Until 2008, money market funds would have been included in that category. But then Bruce Bent, the man who invented the money market fund, saw his own fund, Reserve Primary Fund, "break the buck," or fail to hold the $1-per-share net asset value. So many things that we saw as being tried and true gave way during this economic collapse. But unless you are wealthy to begin with, you will not earn enough in "safe" investments to accomplish your goals. The less money you have, the more important it is for you to take some prudent risks.

How do you approach risk in other aspects of your life? Many people avoid investment risk chiefly because they lack knowledge about investments, yet they shoulder huge financial risks in other areas. Getting married, having children, buying a house, changing jobs, starting a business, moving all carry enormous financial risk.

Learning more about investing is certain to help you feel more comfortable, so get educated. Learn to distinguish between different levels of risk, too. Just because an investment is risky doesn't mean it's good. Some risky investments are just plain foolish. And some people who sell them are looking to make a quick buck at your expense.

Risk and reward go hand in hand. That's one of the first principles of risk. Concentrating on one stock or one segment of the market is risky. It can also be rewarding. So with a bigger potential reward comes the possibility of loss. For example, a mutual fund that invests in just one sector of the market is riskier than one that buys stocks more broadly across different industries.

Remember, too, that time is on your side. Time horizon is one of the biggest factors in determining risk tolerance. If you have ten or twenty or thirty years to invest your money, you can afford to take risks.

You can also expect to see a black swan. Nassim Nicholas Taleb gave the term "black swan" to the rare and hard-to-predict events that make an impact on the market well beyond normal expectations, like the events that occurred during the fall of 2008; they seemed unthinkable until they happened.[1]

But inflation is a risk to our retirement nest eggs, too, and we know that inflation will happen and that the dollars we put away today will be worth only pennies when we plan to spend them unless we invest them to grow at more than the pace of inflation.

---

1. The term "black swan" comes from the underlying assumption "All swans are white"; a black swan was a symbol for something that could not exist. When black swans were discovered in Western Australia in the eighteenth century, what was perceived as an impossibility came to exist.

What Risk?

LIFE IS ABOUT RISK. Creating the life you want for yourself requires risk taking. And it also requires saving. Try to think more broadly about risk in all parts of your life by taking this quiz:

1. You and your spouse are ready to have a child. Both spouses work, but the husband's company announces coming layoffs. You would ...
   a. proceed full steam ahead; you're not getting any younger.
   b. figure that if the husband were to be laid off, he could perform child care duties while thinking about his next career move.
   c. put your family plans on hold for a year while the two of you get the lay of the land.
   d. reconsider having a family; life is too uncertain.

2. Your friend takes you to an early morning sale at a nearby clothing outlet. The prices are great, but you can't try anything on and you can't return anything. You ...
   a. go for broke, buying five suits that you figure cost half what you would pay in a department store.
   b. Choose one $500 item. You saw the same piece of clothing for $1,000 and you're willing to bet that you can alter it if it doesn't fit.
   c. Buy a couple of low-priced items figuring that you'll just lose a little if they don't work out
   d. Spend two hours writing down sizes, prices, and brand names. You plan to go to the local department store and try these items on so that you can come back and buy them, knowing that they will fit.

3. After you make an investment you typically feel
   a. thrilled.
   b. satisfied.

    c. confused.

    d. regretful.

4. It's time to plan you vacation. You

    a. take off on a mystery tour where the destination isn't revealed until you're en route.

    b. discover a small ad in the newspaper for a 50 percent off charter flight to Thailand. You mail in your deposit and delight in your good fortune.

    c. call a trusted travel agent to suggest two or three places that he knows you will like and then pick the most economical of the lot.

    d. don't have to plan because you always vacation at the same spot; you know it will be comfortable.

5. When faced with a major financial decision, you

    a. flip a coin.

    b. go with your gut.

    c. research the options.

    d. call each of your friends and ask for advice.

    e. agonize.

6. You think your boss is brilliant, but with him in charge, you're never going to get anywhere. Then he decides to start his own business and invites you to come along as his No. 2. You

    a. go with him for a pay cut and a share of the company.

    b. demand a higher salary instead of equity in the company.

    c. stay where you are and hope to get his job.

If you picked the first answer to each of these six questions, you are adventuresome indeed—maybe even too much so. Be careful when picking investments not to go overboard. If you picked the final answer to each question, you may sometimes feel virtually paralyzed when making financial decisions. See what you can do to loosen up your thinking a bit. In any case, use these questions to get you thinking about how you approach risk and whether it's working for you in investing—and in your life. We must all take prudent risks in order to improve the quality of our lives. As they say in sports, no pain, no gain.

What Do You Have to Lose/Gain?

YOUR FINANCIAL circumstances affect the risk you can take, too. If you are young and can set your money aside for a long time, you can afford to be aggressive. Knowledge, too, can increase your capacity for risk taking.

1. If your age is ...   Give yourself
   a. under 30   5 points
   b. over 30 and under 40   4 points
   c. over 40 and under 50   3 points
   d. between 50 and 65   2 points
   e. over 65   1 point
2. If your major investment goals are   Give yourself
   a. zero to two years away   1 point
   b. two to five years away   2 points
   c. five to ten years away   3 points
   d. more than ten years away   4 points
3. If your future earning power   Give yourself
   a. keeps pace with inflation, if you're   1 point
      lucky
   b. keeps you a few points ahead of   2 points
      inflation
   c. far exceeds inflation (big bucks ahead)   4 points
   d. includes an expected inheritance or
      some other big chunk of money   5 points
4. Pick the statement that best describes you   Give yourself
   a. I never save or invest.   1 point
   b I do my best to tuck away a few dollars   2 points
      here and there.

c. I save regularly.   3 points

d. I put aside 5 percent of my income no   5 points
   matter what.

5. Give yourself 1 point for each thing you do:

   a. skim the financial pages from time
      to time

   b. read the daily financial news

   c. keep abreast of markets

   d. subscribe or use at least one financial
      Web site

   e. watch investment and financial programs
      on TV

   f. subscribe to an investment newsletter

6. Pick the statement that best describes
   you   Give yourself

   a. I am a knowledgeable investor, able to   5 points
      explain concepts such as standard
      deviation.

   b. I use only mutual funds, but am well   4 points
      versed in the types available and how
      they work.

   c. I have a grasp of the basics such as   2 points
      how the stock and bond markets work.

   d. I hate financial discussions and avoid   0 points
      them at all costs.

If you picked up 18 points or more, you have substantial capacity for risk, including both investment knowledge and financial wherewithal. If you scored 10 to 15, you are in a position to take moderate risk. If you scored 12 or below, be careful: You don't have the time or assets or knowledge yet to tackle more aggressive investments.

Risk Basics

YOU KNOW YOU MUST INVEST. But when you invest, you will encounter special risks to your money that you should understand. Here are the most common ones:

■ ***Risk:** *Inflation, the general and continual increases in the prices of all the things you need to buy, such as food, housing, clothing and medical care.*

■ When you are investing for a long-term goal, like retirement, inflation risk means that the dollars you stash away may be worth just pennies when you're ready to spend them in retirement. You risk losing your money to inflation if you don't invest at all or if the investments you choose don't earn enough to keep pace with inflation, which averages about 3 percent a year over a long period. There have been periods, like the early eighties, when inflation reached 12 percent and others, like the early nineties, when it was under 2 percent a year. During the twenty-first century, it has been in the 3 percent range until the beginning of 2009, when it was around zero.

■ **Antidote:** Find investments that keep pace or beat inflation. When top financial planners build a portfolio for a client, they base the projected return on what they will get after inflation.

■ ***Risk:** *Rising or falling interest rates, which cause the price of many investments to rise or fall suddenly.*

■ Bonds are hardest hit by changes in interest rates. The longer the maturity of the bond, the bigger the impact.

■ **Antidote:** Don't buy and hold long-term bonds. They are suitable for investors who believe that interest rates will fall. Other investors should use short and intermediate term bonds with maturities of less than ten years,

■ ***Risk:** *Default by a borrower or issuer of bonds.*

■ Credit or default risk is the chance that a borrower won't repay. When you buy a bond, you are lending money to the issuer. The greater the credit risk, the greater the interest rate a borrower or issuer of securities must pay. That's why high-yield or "junk" bonds carry the highest interest rates. The mortgage mess of 2008 and 2009 showed us what can happen with junk or even with investment-grade corporate bonds.

■ **Antidote:** Government bonds are guaranteed by the U.S. government. If you are squeamish, stick with Treasuries. Bond funds are a good way to diversify your risk.

■ ***Risk:** *Lost opportunity.*

■ Opportunity risk is the risk that you will tie up your money in a so-so investment and lose the chance to put it into something with real growth potential. Investors who buy long-term bonds or certificates of deposit face this risk. If you buy long-term bonds and prices go up, you have locked in a lower rate.

■ **Antidote:** Limit your exposure to individual or particular risks by diversifying your assets. You're not simply trying to capture gains in different markets. You are trying to balance investments so that you avoid the big losses of putting everything into one market that goes down.

■ ***Risk:** *Concentration—or too many eggs in one basket.*

■ Portfolios with many different kinds of investments carry less risk than those with only a few because the diversification reduces the effects of losses or gains on any particular investment.

■ **Antidote:** Diversify. Advisers tell clients to put assets into different "baskets" like small-cap stocks and large-cap stocks and bonds and cash to cushion the swings in any one market. After the 2009 market plunge, some advisors began to add even more asset classes such as commodities like oil, wheat, metals like gold, and other currencies like Swiss francs.

■ ***Risk:** *That you won't be able to reinvest your earnings at the same rate next month or next year.*

■ If you put $10,000 in a bond that pays 7 percent interest, you will earn $700 a year. But if rates drop, you will not be able to reinvest your $700 at 7 percent.

■ **Antidote:** None.

10

Correlation

ALTHOUGH YOU NEED not be a professional investor to make a good job of investing your 401(k) funds, I think it's worthwhile to look at some of the tools pros use to wring the emotion out of the investment equation. Emotions are a wonderful and necessary thing for a fulfilling life, but they have no part in investing. Most mistakes individual investors make come from emotions like fear and greed or, in the case of 2008 and 2009, sheer terror. Investing is a bit of science and a bit of art, but it should never be emotional. Selling on fear is another way to almost guarantee a loss.

One important investing tool is to examine correlation between different asset classes in your portfolio. Correlation measures the way two securities, mutual funds, or electronically traded funds perform relative to one another. Ideally, you want asset classes that perform well in different market environments. Accomplishing this is increasingly difficult because world markets more often move in tandem today. During the market plunge of 2008, it was impossible to avoid the disaster. Every asset class was hit at the same time, some more than others, true, but nobody escaped. Even careful experts like Ross Levin and his colleagues at Accredited Investors in Minneapolis got caught. Consider that in 2000, when the market lost 50 percent, Levin's client portfolios lost about 11 percent. But during the 2008 to 2009 period when the market lost 50 percent, Levin's portfolios lost 35 percent—better, to be sure, than it could have been, but that's because Levin is a professional investor who has been studying this stuff for most of his life.

So, before you begin to invest your 401(k) money, think about correlation. Holding uncorrelated assets does not guarantee that you will have a cushion and lose less in a market disaster, but it gives you a fighting chance. Holding all your assets in the same category almost sets you up to lose.

Let's assume that you use mutual funds for your 401(k) plan. You don't want two mutual funds that move in lockstep. If two investments move in tandem, professionals refer to that as a perfect correlation of 100 percent, or a correlation coefficient of +1.0. Two investments with a correlation of –1.0 would provide a perfect negative correlation. That would be a great help in building an investment portfolio, if only you could find them. Unfortunately, there are no two investments with a perfect negative correlation.

Yet investors are always on the lookout for investments that behave in different ways in the same environment because such investments decrease the risk in a portfolio. That's because when one asset class takes a dive, another one performs well. "What you want is one investment that zigs when another zags," says Don Phillips at Morningstar, the mutual funds research company.

All correlation measures fall somewhere between the perfect positive of +1.0 and the perfect negative of –1.0. Investment professionals consider investments with a correlation higher than 0.75 to be highly correlated and a poor choice for diversification.

Novice investors typically buy a group of funds with well-known names, believing they have achieved good diversification. Names mean nothing. Large funds are likely to hold the same well-known stocks that are touted by research reports. The bigger a fund is, the more difficult it is to find investments that are off the beaten path. Tiny companies don't have much impact on a giant fund. Consider the Fidelity Magellan Fund, which is still probably the best-known name in mutual funds and the one often selected for 401(k) plans. When I wrote the first version of this book in 1998, Fidelity Magellan had $63 billion in assets. As I revise it in 2009, Magellan contains about $15.53 billion. I think that indicates investors have gained wisdom since the days when Magellan was bought largely for its name recognition rather than its investment record.

This is an important lesson that many investors have learned in the past decade since I first wrote this book on 401(k) plans. Big name funds like Magellan and Janus and Windsor no longer get so many 401(k) plan investors simply because of their names. That doesn't necessarily mean that 401(k) plan investors are not making mistakes. They're making different mistakes, particularly with the introduction of target-date funds, managed accounts, and electronically traded funds, which I'll discuss soon.

More Tools

WHEN I WAS A BEGINNING INVESTOR, I thought the game was to find the investment with the highest possible return. That's what we all want, isn't it? Don Phillips at Morningstar taught me that if two investors assemble portfolios with the same mandate and one earns twice as much, it's because the manager took twice as much risk. If a market index of big-company stocks like the Standard & Poor's 500 Index provides a return of 10 percent over a one-year period and a mutual fund that invests in large-cap stocks returns 25 percent, that portfolio took more risk.

Professional investors use a variety of academic tools to measure risk and to analyze and compare the performance of different stocks and mutual funds. You don't need to employ these tools to invest your 401(k) money well, but I believe it's always an advantage to understand more rather than less. And a better understanding of risk can benefit you. The most common measurement of risk, and perhaps most useful to individual investors, is *standard deviation*, which shows how far the return of a mutual fund might be expected to deviate from its average return, based on its history. Think of a bell curve with the average—or mean—in the middle, and a wide band above and below that average. Statistics tell us that we can expect the returns of a fund to fall within 1 standard deviation from the mean two-thirds of the time. Returns can be expected to fall within 2 standard deviations 95 percent of the time.

For instance, let's say the average, or mean, return for Fund X over a period of three years is 10 percent. The standard deviation is also 10. So one standard deviation encompasses returns from 0 percent to 20 percent; 2 standard deviations range from minus 10 to 30 percent. If you looked at such a fund, you might say that there is almost no chance that you will lose more than 10 percent or gain more than 30 percent in a year with this fund, based on its history.

If the same fund had a standard deviation of 15 percent, the range of your expected returns (assuming 2 standard deviations is your expected range) would fall between –20 percent and 40 percent.

Let's look quickly at the three tools of modern portfolio theory. *Beta* measures risk or the volatility of a fund relative to the market; *alpha* attempts to measure the value added or subtracted by a portfolio manager by showing the performance of a fund relative to the risk it took. And *R-squared* attempts to show how much confidence you can put in a fund's beta and alpha by showing you how similar the fund is to the market. We'll start at the bottom.

R-squared shows the percentage of movement in a particular security or mutual fund that is explained by the movement in an index, ranging from 0 to 100. So a stock or fund that moves in tandem with the S&P 500 would have an R-squared of 100 because 100 percent of its movement is explained by the movement of the S&P. So it is that the Vanguard Index 500 has an R-squared of 100. All of its movement is attributed to changes in the index itself. But very little of the movement of the Japan Fund, for example, is explained by the movement of the S&P index. You might compare SPY to the Japan Fund if you are looking for two investments with a low correlation.

Beta measures the volatility of a fund by comparing its return to the return of a benchmark, which has a beta of 1.0. A fund with a beta of 1.0 tracks the movement of the index exactly. A fund with a beta of 1.25 has 25 percent more volatility. That means you can expect it to rise 25 percent more in an up market and sink 25 percent more in a down market. A fund with a beta of 0.75 is less volatile than the market. You can expect a return 25 percent lower than the overall market when the market goes up and to lose 25 percent less when the market goes down. Of course, these are not guarantees but simply another way to measure risk.

Alpha is an attempt to measure the value a manager adds or subtracts. A positive alpha implies the manager delivered more return than could be expected given the risk that he took. A negative alpha suggests that the portfolio investors were not compensated for the risk.

12

Diversify

ONE OF THE MOST BASIC PIECES of advice to investors is: diversify. Ten years ago, I told 401(k) plan investors that asset allocation—or selecting the right mix of asset classes such as international stocks, small-company stocks, large-company stocks, and bonds—was the key to successful investing. Combining different asset classes allows you to include assets that seem risky by themselves, like small stocks or emerging markets, and still create a portfolio with low volatility because of the correlation between these assets and they way they offset each other. Today, most investment professionals still advocate that strategy.

If you are an experienced investor, go for it. For the rest of us, investing has grown more complex over the past decade, and we may not feel like spending so much time parsing large-company stocks and separating them into core, growth, and value. For better and for worse, many employers who implement 401(k) plans for their employees have simplified the job by offering managed accounts, which means that a professional manager puts together a mix of asset classes and offers it in more and less aggressive flavors. The fastest growing type of fund investment is the target-date fund. The investor chooses the year he hopes to retire and makes that his target-date, such as 2030, and invests in the target-date 2030 fund.

Target-date funds were seen as a nearly miraculous solution to the problems of picking investments for the 401(k) plan, at least until the market disaster that began in 2008 when some of the flaws became apparent. Ron Surz of Target Date Analytics in San Clemente, California, conducts regular research on target-date funds and has written 2009 reports with names like "The Target-Date Emperor Has No Clothes" because his research showed that the closest-in funds, the 2010s, had lost considerable assets during the crash, just when investors who planned retirement in 2010 needed their assets.

We'll discuss target-date funds on p. 162. In this section on diversification, I'll repeat traditional asset-allocation wisdom that's still relevant. For investors with a long time horizon, stocks should represent the bulk of the portfolio. To determine how much, think again about your risk tolerance. Stocks have the highest average annual return over time but the path is bumpy. Adding bonds and/ or cash to your portfolio cushions the ride. A portfolio of 60 percent stocks and 40 percent bonds is a typical mix and is roughly the make up of funds called "balanced funds."

But what if you've got the tolerance for risk and you want to go for the highest return? Many professional investors put 100 percent of their personal portfolios in stocks. Yet some studies show there is little extra to be gained with the final 15 percent. In other words, a long-term portfolio that is 85 percent in stocks and 15 percent in short-term bonds or cash might be ideal for an aggressive investor because it would provide market returns with a small cushion against market volatility. As I mentioned earlier, some financial advisors suggested even broader diversification in 2009, including assets such as gold, energy, currencies like the Swiss franc, and Treasury Inflation Protected Securities (TIPS). The principal of a TIPS bond increases with inflation and decreases with deflation, as measured by the consumer price index (CPI). When a TIPS matures, you are paid the adjusted principal or original principal, whichever is greater.

In the mid-1990s, the large company stocks that make up the major market indexes like the Dow Jones Industrials and the S&P 500 raced ahead, gaining 37 percent in 1995 and another 23 percent in 1996. The easiest, and worst, strategy is to be a follower, investing in a particular sector just as it eases off from big recent gains. The shifting fortunes of different investment categories prove the benefit of including each of them. Do not wait until a particular asset class takes off to get on the bandwagon. If you do, you miss out on much of the upswing.

A final word here about diversification: Investing in funds with different names does not mean you are diversifying. Fund names mean nothing. A great example of that is the once wildly popular Magellan Fund. Based on the investment prowess of its initial manager, Peter Lynch, this fund soared in assets to over $100 billion in 1999, long after Lynch was gone. To investors in the roaring bull market of the 1990s, the Magellan name was magic. The fund was not. Managing such a huge pile of assets and managing it well in hard times is virtually impossible. In 2009, the fund had shrunk to $15 billion.

Why Stocks?

YOU KNOW by now why you should buy stocks: they represent the investment with the greatest growth potential. If you rode through the bear market of 2007 to 2009, you probably know why you shouldn't buy stocks: They represent the investment with a great potential for loss. Studying the stock market can be a lifetime job, as it is for many professionals. Even if you are just a novice, you probably understand that *no one* really knows when the market will go up or why and when it might head down. Hundreds of theories exist on what moves the markets and when and how to invest.

Yet if you followed the market on October 27, 1987, when it plummeted by 554 points and then gained 337 points the following day, you probably see the mystery in the movements of the market. Or what about more recent history, like the first quarter of 2009? The Dow Jones Industrials Average hit a twelve-year low of 6,469.95 on March 9 and then gained 21 percent in the following thirteen trading days to close at 7,924.56 on March 26. A bull market is defined as a rise of 20 percent from the recent bottom. According to common Wall Street definition, this was the fastest 20 percent rebound from a bear market low since 1938.

Don't make the mistake of thinking that you must understand all this stuff in order to be an investor. Think of it like peeling an onion: Peel off as many or as few layers as you like. The number of layers you choose and the amount of time you want to spend with the onion determine what kind of investor you will be.

If investing doesn't interest you and you don't want to spend much time, one layer is enough. You need to know that stocks represent equity in a company. When you buy stock, you become a part owner of that business. Your fortunes become those of the companies you own. You share in their prosperity and your investment suffers during their hard times.

Most companies, particularly the large ones, pay dividends on their common stock. If the company has a great year, it may raise the dividend and the share price may go up. If the company is sued—or taken over by the federal government—the share price might nosedive.

Consider Bank of America stock, which traded at 40.65 on May 2, 2008 and sunk to 2.53 on February 20, 2009. Because the fortunes of a single company are difficult for any investor to predict, most investors choose to invest in a mutual fund or an exchange-traded fund (ETF) and choose a manager to do the analysis and pick the companies.

Professionals debate endlessly about the efficiency of the market. An "efficient" market would quickly correct inaccuracies in the pricing of securities. So, if a stock traded too low, investors would snap it up; if it traded too high, investors would sell. An efficient market would constantly right itself like a finely calibrated scale. The more efficient the market, the fewer the opportunities to make money. But the truth is that plenty of pockets of inefficiency exist. Not all information about a company is available to all investors. If the market were truly efficient, if there were no money to be made—or lost—by surprises, what can we say about the market crash of 1987? Of 2000? Or 2008? In the last crash, plenty of investors lost money, and some of them were mutual fund managers with thirty years experience. Very few made money.

The vagaries of investor psychology create the chief reason for inefficiencies. Richard Thaler, professor of economics at the University of Chicago's Booth School of Business and one of the first economists to make an argument for "behavioral finance," or market movement determined by the behavior of crowds, put it this way: If everyone investing in the market were totally rational, no stock would ever be bought or sold. If someone wanted to sell 100 shares of IBM, no one would buy it precisely because he wanted to sell.

Of course, not everyone investing in the market is rational. Professionals believe that individual investors like you and me are particularly irrational. That's why they devised many contrarian tools to help them invest in a manner *opposite* to what we do.

Key to investing in stocks is to avoid making irrational decisions. That's it. If you want to peel just one layer off the onion, simply resolve that you will not be irrational; that you will not second guess yourself and pull out of the market when it sinks. Thaler often says the perfect investor resembles Rip Van Winkle. He invests and then goes to sleep for twenty years. If that's you, index funds are probably the best investment because they simply follow an index and require no active management decisions. If you want to peel another layer, read on.

Index Funds

IF YOU ARE A MATHEMATICIAN or an engineer, you're going to love this. If you're an artist or an English major, it's worth your trouble to see it through. An index fund—or a passively managed fund—invests in all the stocks that make up a particular index or in a sampling of those stocks. Once invested, the fund is passive, simply holding the stocks. No active manager picks and chooses stocks or receives a fee for management. Fees are low. A good index fund moves up and down with the market. The Vanguard Index Trust charges 18 percent of 1 percent, or 18 basis points, in expenses. That compares to 1.19 percent or 119 basis points, for the industry average, according to Lipper Analytical Services.

Passive management grew out of the work in efficient market theory of a number of economists in the 1960s. John C. Bogle, founding chairman of the Vanguard Group, explains efficient market theory this way in his books:

All investors together own the entire stock market. Passive investors as a group will match the gross return of the overall market because they are invested in all the stocks. So, active investors, as a group, can do no better. They, too, must simply match the market.

Because the fees and transaction costs incurred by the passive investors are much lower than those paid by active investors, and both groups get the same gross returns, it follows that passive investors will get the higher *net* returns. Indeed, active managers must beat the market by 2 percentage points just to come out *even* after paying expenses.

Yes, I hear you saying, but active managers as a group include some good managers and some bad managers. You are going to choose the good ones—the ones that beat the average—while I choose the losers. Bogle concedes that a handful of excellent managers outperform the market, people like, for instance, Warren Buffett. But, he says, such extraordinary managers not only are few in number but are difficult to identify in advance. Not only that, but the recent market debacle did something to bring down the giants, too. Consider this: A $20.50 investment in Buffett's Berkshire Hathaway fund in 1967 when it opened would have grown to $141,600 at the end of 2007, an annualized return of 24.73 percent over the fund's first forty years. But in 2008, Berkshire lost 32.1 percent, it worst annual loss by far. And in the first half of 2009, it lost another 7.5 percent. Will it regain its footing? Who knows?

Bogle cites academic studies that show that only two in five stock mutual funds outperform the market over time and only one in five does so once sales charges are taken into account. The performance of active managers is inconsistent, and it is usually not the same ones who outperform from year to year.

When the studies on passive management were done in the 1960s, big institutional investors like pension funds immediately recognized their merits. The first institutional index fund was opened in 1971, and billions of dollars poured into these funds throughout the 1970s. The first retail index fund, the Vanguard 500 Index, set up by Bogle in 1976, had a tougher row to hoe. The indexing story lacked romance and passion—the two emotions that lure fickle individual investors like us. Bogle's fund began to grow in the 1980s as these investors began to see the logic of passive investing. In 1995 and 1996, money poured into the fund, bringing it to number two in size behind Magellan and putting the index fund in the unlikely position of the "hot fund" of the year.

Much of this money came into the fund for the wrong reason. Many new shareholders did not understand that an index fund moves up and down along with the index with a slight difference for expenses. These investors selected the Index 500, because they thought it "hot" rather than for the mathematical reasons outlined by Bogle in his many books, such as *Common Sense on Mutual Funds* (a revised and updated edition is due out November 2009). Many of the investors who piled into the Index 500 in the mid-nineties merely saw that Bogle's once-ignored index fund was outperforming most other funds.

Today, mutual funds are available on hundreds of indexes. In the spring of 2009, Vanguard brought out an international small-cap index fund, Vanguard® FTSE All-World ex-US Small-Cap Index Fund (VSS), intended to track the investment performance of small company stocks around the world, excluding those in the United States. This Vanguard investment is an exchange-traded fund (ETF). Nearly all ETFs are index funds. More about them coming up in section 23 of this chapter.

15

Active Funds

THOUSANDS OF HOURS are spent debating the merits of passive management—investing in a static portfolio that is usually designed to mimic a market index—versus active management—active security selection by a money manager. Most of these debates focus on the academic arguments for one versus the other. In fact, the issue is largely one of individual style. Remember the discussion on behavioral finance on p. 124?

Ross Levin, a financial planner from Minneapolis, said it best when he introduced a panel on active versus passive management at a financial planning conference. Levin said that he uses actively managed funds because he enjoys doing the research to find the funds. Active managers are more interesting to him and more interesting to his clients. Maybe they want to know which sports team the fund manager supports or his favorite restaurant. "Active managers keep my clients interested and keep them in the investment game," Levin said. Yet he acknowledged that if he preferred passive management he would no doubt attract clients who prefer passive funds. "What I think really matters is that you believe in what you're doing and have passion for it," Levin said.

Intellectually the argument for indexing is a strong one. I suspect most professionals accept it, as do most amateurs like me. Yet each and every one of us secretly believes that our guy will be the one to beat the odds.

Consider Burton G. Malkiel, author of *A Random Walk Down Wall Street*, a friend of John Bogle, and a great advocate of indexing. In his book, he explains that because the markets are efficient, most active managers fall behind the market index. Yet Malkiel uses active funds himself. He also argues that investing can be fun. "A successful investor is generally a well-rounded individual who puts a natural curiosity and an intellectual interest to work to earn more money." That means picking active managers. Paul Samuelson, the Nobel laureate economist whose work was instrumental in the development of index funds, invests in Berkshire Hathaway, the company run by Warren Buffett, the best-known investor of our time. Even Vanguard's Bogle buys some actively managed funds.

There's really no contradiction here. As Malkiel says in his book, the fun of investing is to pit your intellect "against that of the vast investment community and to find yourself rewarded with an increase in assets." I won't be pitting my intellect against the vast investment community. But I've certainly had my share of actively managed funds, including a few value funds I sold recently because they were worth less than I paid for them ten years ago. But I could make the argument that, even if you did no better than the index, or slightly worse, it still might make sense for you to use active managers if that helps you learn about investing and keeps you in the market. In other words, if it helps soften those two investing emotions (fear and greed) that too often pull us into the market or push us out without any mathematical underpinnings at all and at the very worst time.

So there is no right and wrong. How do you feel about your investing? What will help you to hang in there? If your eyes glaze over at the thought of reading the *Wall Street Journal*, if you'd rather be listening to the opera or country music, stick to passive investing. If you can't wait to tuck in with a cup of tea and *Outstanding Investor Digest*, you're going to be bored by index funds. Study up on active managers.

Of course, index funds and active funds need not be mutually exclusive. Think of it as a continuum, ranging from investors who index their entire portfolio, to those who use index funds as a core and selects active funds to complement them, to those—like Morningstar managing director Don Phillips—who use all active managers. Could it have anything to do with the fact that Phillips did graduate work in literature at the University of Chicago and planned to become a college professor? I think so. Phillips likes a dollop of romance with his investing choices. We all fit in somewhere along the continuum, based chiefly on the passion each of us has for investing and our risk tolerance.

16

Investment Style

NOT SO LONG AGO, investors were advised to buy funds based on the fund's objective, such as "aggressive growth" or "income" or "growth and income." But the labels were broad and confusing. Two aggressive growth funds were likely to pursue two entirely different strategies in search of growth.

As investors have grown more sophisticated, they've begun to look at funds based on the manager's investment style. By style, I mean chiefly two things: What size companies does the fund buy, and what method does it use to select them? You should keep investment style in mind as you invest your 401(k) portfolio as well.

The two key investment styles used by stock investors are value and growth. Value investors look for companies with a hidden value not reflected in the stock price. That's done in myriad ways. *Outstanding Investor Digest*, an excellent newsletter for the real hard-core investors, devotes more than sixty-five pages in each issue to exploring the ways investors like Warren Buffett of Berkshire Hathaway make investment decisions. I interviewed Henry Emerson, editor of this quirky publication some years ago. Like most people who put together a serious publication based on their passion—and maybe their search for truth—Emerson is a fascinating guy, perhaps a genius, who lives and breathes value investing.

Some of his investors might poke around in bankruptcy filings. Many look for companies that hold assets like real estate that could be sold for a gain. They look at comparable companies in the same industry to get an idea of a stock's potential. Most look for some catalyst, like a new chief executive, that might unlock the hidden value in a company. Many value investors like companies with a low price/earnings (P/E) ratio. The P/E ratio shows the relationship of the stock price to earnings. It could be last year's earnings, this year's earnings, or projected earnings. No formula is foolproof. One value investor, John Gunn, co-manager of Dodge & Cox Stock, looks for cheap stocks and adds to positions when prices fall. He also likes financials, so when companies like American International Group (AIG) and Fannie Mae began to slide in late 2008, he loaded up on these stocks. But this time financials did much worse than the rest of the market. At least for the end of 2008 and into 2009, the market had changed drastically and seemed to have thrown out all the rules. "Like Dorothy in *The Wizard of Oz*, we weren't in Kansas anymore," Gunn told the *Wall Street Journal* in April 2009. "Well let's sit on the sidelines and watch this game a little bit."[2]

Growth investors don't care about any of this stuff. They believe that rapidly rising corporate earnings are the single most important factor driving stock prices. Many of them don't care at all about measures that seem to indicate that a company is overpriced by some traditional valuation. They look for growth!

Some growth managers are called *momentum* investors because they buy stocks based on earnings momentum. They might use a computer program, for example, to look for "earnings surprises," or those companies that report earnings higher than the consensus of Wall Street estimates. Some growth managers claim they do not even know what business their companies operate in.

Academics have done considerable research to try to determine which investment style is more successful—value or growth. What they've concluded is that both do well in different market environments. If you are using actively managed funds, consider including both investment styles.

Morningstar Mutual Funds categorizes funds based on investment style. In addition to value and growth styles, Morningstar looks at company size. A great deal of evidence shows that small companies have more growth potential over time than big, well-established companies. Many small companies also fail. Small-company stocks run in cycles; they outperform during some periods and underperform in others. So a diversified portfolio would include large-company and small-company growth and large-company and small-company value. Many 401(k) plans now offer managed target-date funds or managed accounts so that someone else makes these decisions for you. But you can't assume that their decisions are always correct.

---

2. Shefali Anand and Karen Damato, "What the Past Teaches Us about Today," *Wall Street Journal*, April 6, 2009, http://online.wsj.com/article/SB123862046764979775.html.

Bonds

A BOND IS A LOAN. If you go to a bank to borrow money, the bank looks over your credit history and decides whether to offer you a loan. The banker also decides what interest rate you will pay. If your credit is immaculate, you may get a lower rate. If you are a bad risk, you probably won't get a loan at all, or you will end up borrowing money wherever you can get it, probably at a very high interest rate. When you take out the loan, you agree to pay a predetermined rate of interest and to repay the loan over a specified period of time.

When a large institution wants to borrow money, it may go to a bank the same way you do to make a loan. Or it may decide instead to borrow from investors by issuing a bond. Part of that decision is based on the level of interest rates. If they are low, the institution might want to lock in the low rate for a long term—just like you do when you take out a mortgage on your home—by issuing a bond.

Bonds are the debt of corporations and government agencies. When you invest in a bond, you are making a loan to the bond's issuer. The issuer promises to pay you a set rate of interest, which is sometimes called the *coupon*. The issuer also agrees to repay the principal at a specific time. (You probably repay your bank loan in installments. The issuer of a bond typically repays in a single lump sum at maturity.)

Your concern as a bond investor should be the same as those of the bank that loans you money. First is the ability or willingness of the issuer to repay the money. Bonds are assigned letter grades by Moody's Investor Service and Standard & Poor's Corporation that are supposed to indicate their creditworthiness.

Unfortunately, the rules of the bond game changed over the last ten years with the housing bubble and the subprime mortgages. Wall Street packaged these subprime loans, threw them into a big pot, and issued securities backed by this pot of subprime loans in a process referred to as securitization. The pot of loans was split into several tranches, or portions, based on creditworthiness. The interest rate was very low and the standards for qualifying were very low; teaser rates lured buyers who couldn't afford the loan even at these low rates. These tranches were then rated by the credit agencies, which typically gave the top tranch a high rating, perhaps a triple A rating. When interest rates went up and thousands of buyers of subprime loans defaulted, the entire pot of mortgages began to go bad and fall into default, the triple A as well as the lower-rated loans. The ratings for large corporations were no more reliable. American International Group (AIG) carried a triple A rating when it traded at $75 a share and it carried a triple A rating when it traded for pennies a share. The ratings became meaningless when triple A-rated companies like AIG began to fail and to require huge government bailouts if they were to continue to operate. The rating agencies have come under well-deserved fire for their tax ratings. The safest bonds are those issued by the U.S. government because they are backed by the full faith and credit (and the taxing power) of the government itself.

If you stick with government bonds, you avoid credit risk—the risk that the issuer will default. But you still face interest-rate risk, or the effect of a change in interest rates on your bond investment. Because the interest rate on your bond is locked in, the market price of your bond—what you can sell it for on the open market—will fluctuate to reflect the change in interest rates. When interest rates rise, the price of the bond you hold falls.

The point of investing in bonds is to add ballast to your portfolio. Expected return on bonds over the long term is lower than that for stocks, so the reason to add them is to diversify your portfolio. That hasn't worked at the beginning of the twenty-first century. Will it work again later? Maybe.

The safest bonds are *Treasury Inflation Protected Securities* or *TIPS*, which carry the backing of the U.S. government as well as protection against inflation. The principal of a TIPS bond increases with inflation and decreases with deflation, as measured by the consumer price index (CPI). When TIPS mature, they pay the adjusted principal or the original principal, whichever is greater.

18

International Investing

THERE WAS A TIME WHEN U.S. stocks represented two-thirds of the value of all the stocks trading in the world. By the end of the twentieth century, though, the numbers flip-flopped, and two-thirds of the value of all stocks was to be found outside the United States, so experts argued that the best way to diversify and cut risk while increasing return was to invest 30 to 40 percent of a U.S. stock portfolio overseas; that way, one investment will zig as the other zags. Many Americans began to invest in foreign stocks both to diversify their holdings and to create potential for portfolio.

But can you pick foreign stocks? How about stocks in India or Australia? I certainly can't. Nor can most portfolio managers. This is where exchange-traded funds (ETF) come in handy. These funds, which are just now being introduced in 401(k) plans, allow investors to pick a particular sector of the economy or a specific geographical region or both.

You can buy an index of foreign stocks just as you buy an index of U.S. stocks. One way to compare investment returns is to look at the Standard & Poor's Index of 500 Stocks (the ETF is SPY) and the EAFE or Europe, Australasia and Far East Index, as a proxy for stocks in developed countries other than the United States. (The iShares MSCI EAFE index is EFA.) Many different ETFs are available that provide indexes for emerging markets such as Egypt, India, Israel, Chile, and South Africa.

The iShares ETFs, managed by Barclays Global Investors, N.A., based on the MSCI indexes, are the leading player in this market, followed by State Street Global Advisors. But Vanguard Group, the birthing company of the retail index fund, has been moving aggressively into index ETFs. And other players, such as Wisdom Tree, have also entered the market.

Today, you can take an investing slice based on energy or technology or health care, for example, and invest it around the globe with a global technology fund like iShares S&P Global Technology Sector Index Fund (IXN).

During the market crash in 2008, geographical diversification did not do international investors much good when markets around the world collapsed at the same time. Indeed, international markets, and even the emerging markets in developing countries, do not provide the cushion against U.S. market downdrafts as they once did. Consider the group of G-20 countries that met at the end of September 2009. The leaders of these 20 nations talked about making economic advances as a team, which would further blunt an effort to diversify a portfolio by investing abroad.

There is another reason for—and another risk involved in—using international funds and that is currency risk. When you invest in foreign funds, your U.S. dollars are converted to the currency of the fund you choose. When you sell the fund, you must convert your investment back to U.S. dollars. This currency translation gives you a gain on that part of your investment if the currency you invest in has gained against the dollar and vice versa.

In the autumn of 2009, the U.S. dollar was falling against other currencies. Some experts say that the long-term outlook for the dollar is not good because of the huge debt the U.S. government is running up.

And, the *Wall Street Journal* reported on September 27, 2009,[3] that, on the heels of one of the worst years in stock-market history, some experts are recommending emerging markets because the developed countries are too debt ridden to grow. The MSCI Emerging Market index was up 60 percent year to date, while the Dow Jones Industrial Average posted a gain of only 10 percent, the *Journal* reported.

If foreign stock funds seem too risky, one alternative is to invest in non-dollar sovereign bonds issued by the central bank of a foreign country. Another possibility is an ETF that invests in bonds issued by the central banks of several foreign countries. One such fund (WIP) invests in inflation protected bonds of countries excluding the U.S.

Yet another option is to invest in a foreign currency through an exchange-traded fund such as FXF (CurrencyShares Swiss Franc Trust), which invests in Swiss franc-denominated bank deposits.

---

3. *Wall Street Journal,* online.wsj.com, http://online.wsj.com/article/SB125399713181243611 .html?mod=WSJ_hpp_MIDDLENexttoWhatsNewsThird.

19

Money Markets

THERE WAS A TIME WHEN PEOPLE referred to cash and meant the coins jingling in their pockets or the bills squirreled away in the cookie jar. During the Great Depression of the 1930s, cash meant one thing: cold hard currency that you could count on, something you could spend in the next fifteen minutes to buy a cup of coffee and a doughnut. Even money in the bank wasn't cash in the 1930s. But after Franklin D. Roosevelt signed the Banking Act of 1933 and created the Federal Deposit Insurance Corporation (FDIC), which put a government guarantee behind bank deposits, Americans gradually began to accept banks. Then bank accounts, too, became "cash."

Our definition of cash continued to change, and it changed radically in the 1970s when "cash" as we know it today was actually invented by Bruce Bent, who was casting about for a business idea. Bent hit upon a plan to collect money from depositors and loan it out to corporations at a slightly higher rate than he paid depositors. Bent figured he could offer a higher rate than a bank because of lower overhead. Because he ran into an obstacle in bank regulation, he decided to use a mutual fund format. His mutual fund would accept money from depositors and use it to make short-term loans to government and big corporations in the money markets, just as a bank does. His profit would come from charging depositors a management fee.

In November 1971, the Securities and Exchange Commission (SEC) approved Bent's registration for the Reserve Primary Fund, the first money market mutual fund. Money market mutual funds invest in short-term debt or short-term "paper," issued by the U.S. Treasury, state and local governments, banks, and large corporations. The SEC mandated that the average maturity of a money market portfolio be 120 days or fewer and that the fund invest only in the top two grades of debt as rated by Standard & Poor's Corporation or Moody's Investor Service. Because these investments were thought to be so stable, money funds offered a fixed share price rather than one that fluctuates from day to day like a mutual fund. The fund was designed so that the share price remained at $1 and the fund could promise preservation of your principal plus a market rate of interest.

The fear of a fund "breaking the buck"—or allowing the asset value to drop below $1—had mostly been extinguished over more than thirty-five years of success for the funds. In 1990, ten money market fund sponsors were forced to back up the "promise" of their funds to keep the net asset value (NAV) steady at $1. Another fifteen funds were bailed out by their sponsors in the early 1990s. Because the fund sponsors prevented these funds from "breaking the buck," consumers retained their confidence in the integrity of the $1 per share net asset value.

In September 2008, Bruce Bent's Reserve Primary Fund, the original money market fund, collapsed because it couldn't make up for the money it lost on debt it held from the failed Lehman Brothers. Investors lost confidence and pulled more than $200 billion out of money funds within two weeks. The nearly $4 trillion money market fund industry stabilized, thanks to government intervention and guarantees, but the low-interest rate climate in 2009 squeezes the funds at the same time it makes them less attractive to investors because they offer only a fraction of a percentage point in interest.

Because the money funds are both costly and risky for mutual fund companies some of them are rethinking the money fund and deciding to drop it or revise the rules. Various government proposals suggest revising the rules so that money funds have a target value rather than the $1 a share "must-hold" value.

In a column in the February 15, 2009, issue of *Investment News*, Robert Gordon, chief executive of Twenty-First Securities Corporation, predicted the disappearance of money funds. "If the risks of money market funds are deemed too great by the nation's new economic leaders, and if the economics of the funds in today's low-interest-rate environment don't change, don't be surprised if money market funds as we know them fade into financial history," Gordon wrote.[4] Like so many other financial instruments, money market funds have been viewed with suspicion by investors after the financial collapse of 2008 and 2009. For now, though, they still represent a safe investment in cash. The funds that invest in U.S. Treasury securities are safest. And don't look for the money fund that offers the highest rate, because that means it is taking bigger risks. In money funds, look for low costs and lower yields rather than higher yields because this combination represents safety.

---

4. Robert Gordon, "Say Goodbye to Money Funds," *Investment News*, February 15, 2009.

Investing in Gold

YOUR 401(K) PLAN PROBABLY does not offer an option for investing in gold. Still, because gold was talked up so much after the 2008-2009 market crash, and because investors in gold seem to be the only ones who didn't lose their shirts, you may be curious about gold as an investment.

Here's the story behind gold: Gold has its own fan club, a group of fervent believers dubbed "goldbugs," who think it is the only true source of value and the time is always right to own it, no matter what time it is. Reality doesn't support this notion. The price of gold was fixed at $35 an ounce in the U.S. from 1934 to 1971. Individuals were prohibited from owning it. When the fixed price was lifted, the price tripled in only two years. In 1974, the ban against private ownership was also lifted and private speculation drove the price still higher, to about $200 an ounce. The price fell back to the $170 range until the roaring inflation of the 1970s when it skyrocketed, hitting $875 an ounce on January 21, 1980. When inflation cooled, the prince of gold dropped back to the $300 to $500 range.

But the price has been rising since 2006, probably because of investor worries about inflation and a falling dollar. Gold first broke through the $1,000 per ounce level in March 2008 and then again in February 2009. It traded above $1,000 an ounce again on September 8, 2009, but dropped back below $1,000 at the day's close.

As this history shows, the price of gold is volatile and largely unpredictable. It is not a growth investment, like stocks or real estate, which increase gradually, albeit unpredictably, over time. In fact, there is an old saw that throughout history an ounce of gold would buy a decent man's suit. During Roman times, it bought a toga. And more recently, it bought a decent business suit. That doesn't bode much for it as a long-term investment strategy.

But gold can make a good hedge against expectations about rising inflation and a falling dollar. Because of the uncertainty in the market in 2008 and 2009, many investors moved to gold, or made a flight to safety. In 2009, some financial advisors recommended gold for a small part of an investor portfolio (approximately 5 percent).

Below is a graph that compares an investor who put $1,000 into gold at the beginning of 1999 to one who put $1,000 into stocks as measured by the Standard & Poor's 500 Index.

Dec 31,	S&P 500	Gold bullion
1999	$1,195.30	$1,005.37
2000	$1,074.97	$944.07
2001	$944.56	$957.40
2002	$720.23	$1,186.80
2003	$897.11	$1,444.76
2004	$976.33	$1,508.30
2005	$1,022.02	$1,776.30
2006	$1,155.09	$2,201.16
2007	$1,209.03	$2,896.45
2008	$731.10	$3,105.16

What does it mean? It means that the past ten years were a much better time to be invested in gold than in stocks. Had I looked instead at the prior ten years, stocks would have done much better than gold. So there is a case for incorporating gold as a small part of a diversified portfolio.

21

Dollar-Cost Averaging (DCA)

SUCCESSFUL INVESTING is all about discipline: discipline in buying and discipline in selling. The best way to discipline yourself is with a systematic investment program in which you make regular monthly or quarterly investments no matter what is happening in the market.

What better way to do this than with your 401(k) plan? You decide at the beginning of the year how much you want deducted from your paycheck; that amount is automatically invested, based on your instructions, at regular intervals throughout the year.

Making automatic investments at regular intervals allows you to take advantage of a "strategy" called dollar-cost averaging (DCA), a bit of investment jargon with a simple meaning: You invest the same amount of money at regular intervals no matter what happens in the market. DCA allows investors to avoid guessing whether the market is going up or down. Your dollars buy more shares when the price goes down and less when it goes up. This strategy helps you spread your risk by paying varying prices for shares of the same stock or fund. Studies show that investors who use dollar-cost averaging tend to pay less per share over time than those who purchase shares in a lump sum.

DCA works particularly well for buying volatile funds because the same $100 buys more shares when the fund's price is down and fewer when it's up. Left to our own decisions, most of us tend to do just the opposite: We buy a fund when it's "hot" and trading at a high and dump it when the price sags, locking in our losses. The better way, of course, is to have confidence in the investment we chose and to continue adding dollars.

Personal finance writers, particularly in the 1990s, were rarely rewarded for writing about dollar-cost averaging or any other simple, supposedly "tried-and-true" method of investing. Instead, the rewards came from debunking these boring and predictable investment strategies. Editors wanted contrarian advice, something with punch, for all those readers waiting to make their million in the stock market. So in that decade, we saw a lot of articles criticizing dollar-cost averaging.

One of the criticisms was written by Timothy Middleton, my former colleague from MSN Money and someone I respect as a writer and reporter. Middleton's column argues that the adage that "Dollar-cost averaging helps you avoid investing too much when the market is high, too little when the market is low," is bunk. How could so many knowledgeable investors disagree so much on what seems a simple strategy?

I found the answer in Middleton's column where he says, "Dollar-cost averaging is similar to, but not the same thing as investing regularly scheduled amounts, such as contributions from every paycheck to a 401(k) plan. It's the alternative to investing a lump sum, such as an inheritance or an IRA rollover, typically over four calendar quarters." In other words, people who talk about DCA mean two different things. Many investors criticize the decision to invest a lump sum over a period of time, such as one year. Even that criticism seemed rash in 2009 when the markets exhibited irrational behavior. Suppose you inherited a half million dollars in 2009. With the market, as measured by the Dow Jones Industrial Average trading in a range from around 6,500 to nearly 10,000, you might have been nervous to dump your entire nest egg in on one day.

But investors in a 401(k) plan do not make a decision about whether to dollar-cost average by depositing the same sum at regular intervals instead of investing the lump all at one time. You simply sign up and indicate how much you want to contribute. That amount is automatically deducted from your paycheck and you will get the benefit of DCA or buying more shares when the price is down, less when it's up without giving it a thought. That discipline to keep pumping money into your investments when the market tanks like it did in September 2008 would serve us well. I doubt if I was the only individual investor who made no investments in early 2009 even as the market moved lower and lower. If I had a system set up to invest regularly every month, my portfolio might look a whole lot better today.

Mutual Funds

MORE THAN 50 MILLION AMERICAN HOUSEHOLDS, 44 percent, own mutual funds, according to the Investment Company Institute (ICI), the mutual fund trade group. Yet surveys show that most Americans still do not know what a mutual fund is or how it works.[5]

Since 1990, retirement plans at work have become one of the most common sources through which individuals invest in mutual funds. Indeed, many of today's mutual fund owners were introduced to mutual fund investing through 401(k) plans and other retirement plans at work. In 2007, 57 percent of households that owned mutual funds said they purchased their first fund through an employer-sponsored retirement plan, up from 47 percent in 1998, according to the ICI. In total, 24 percent of households' mutual fund holdings are held in employer-sponsored retirement plan accounts. About half of households that own mutual funds view these plans as their main fund purchase source.

A mutual fund pools the money of hundreds or thousands or even millions of different investors and invests it in stocks, bonds, money market instruments, and other securities. Each fund sets its own rules. The money each individual invests is pooled with that of all the other investors and used to purchase securities.

Thousands of mutual funds are available, each with a stated investment objective. That objective might be, "This fund seeks current income," which means the fund is designed for investors who need regular income from their investments, such as retirees who live off the income; or it might be "this fund seeks capital appreciation," which means it is designed for investors who hope for long-term growth in their money.

To accomplish the objective, the fund company hires a professional money manager to make investment decisions, trade securities, and accomplish the fund's objective. The prospectus outlines the way the manager plans to accomplish the objective.

Think of a mutual fund as a big pie cut into thin slices. Each slice is called a "share." Each share is allotted a portion of the fund's

5. Investment Company Institute Research Series, "Profile of Mutual Fund Shareholders," fall 2004.

gains, losses, and income, and each share pays a portion of the fund's expenses.

Each investor decides how much to invest—$2,000 or $5,000 or $10,000—and buys a specific number of shares. If a fund trades at $10 per share, $1,000 buys 100 shares. The share price of $10 is called the net asset value (NAV).

Every day the mutual fund company calculates the value of all the assets in the portfolio and deducts the expenses—which include management fees, administrative costs, advertising expenses, and the servicing fees used to pay brokers and others who service the account. The remaining assets are divided by the number of shares outstanding to come up with the value of a single share or the net asset value (NAV). You can still look up the value of your fund in some morning newspapers, although much better information is usually available online. A fund company is obligated to buy and sell shares at the current price, or net asset value (NAV), on every business day, although some funds add sales charges or redemption fees. The fund is bought or sold at the price at the market close. Some fund companies set earlier times—such as 2 p.m.—to order a buy or sell at that day's closing price. As securities trading has increased and attracted many more investors, this delay between price at the time of the order to buy a fund and the actual price of sale, established after trading ends for the day, has become an inconvenience to some investors. (That inconvenience has fueled the growth of exchange-traded funds (ETFs), which can be bought and sold at any time throughout the trading day.) Mutual funds pass on all their gains or losses to the shareholders. The shareholders receive two types of income from mutual fund investments: dividends and capital gains. They pay taxes on this income as if they own the securities outright.

Mutual funds offer numerous advantages for investors: professional management, instant diversification, and convenience. They are easy to buy and sell even in your 401(k) plan. The trend is for 401(k) plan sponsors to offer daily trading. Mutual funds offer flexibility and variety, with hundreds of different choices available.

Of course, most 401(k) plans don't allow you to pick from all the mutual funds, which is probably just as well. Your employer's job is to offer you a range of funds in your plan from which you can construct a portfolio.

23

Exchange-Traded Funds (ETFs)

EXCHANGE-TRADED FUNDS (ETFs) resemble the open-end mutual funds just discussed but with a couple of important differences. ETFs, too, contain a basket of stocks sliced up into individual shares. But unlike mutual funds, they trade on a stock exchange so they can be bought and sold all day—a very attractive feature over the first quarter of 2009 with markets fluctuating wildly over a day. Mutual funds can be bought and sold only at the closing share price at the end of the day. Some fund companies require a buy or sell order by 2 p.m. in order to get that day's price.

Suppose the market seemed to be on a rising trend and you ordered the sale of a mutual fund at 2 p.m., hoping that the rally would hold until your shares are sold after 4 p.m. Then the market tanks in the last two hours, losing 300 points. That happens, and when it does, it could have a disastrous effect on the price you get for your fund. With an ETF, you can order a buy or a sell when you see a rally take hold or at a new market low. Although I don't advocate frequent trading when I do decide to buy or sell an investment, I like to be able to choose the time to do it.

The first ETF—a broad-based domestic equity fund (SPY) tracking the S&P 500—was introduced in 1993. SPY provided an investment nearly identical to the Vanguard S&P 500 Index, the first index fund. The differences were those just outlined in the differences between open-end mutual funds and ETFs. At the end of 2008, there were 728 ETFs holding $531.3 billion in total assets, according to the Investment Company Institute (ICI), the mutual fund industry trade group. The ICI said that ETFs had net inflows of $177.2 billion in 2008 while stock mutual funds had net outflows of $234.3 billion in the same year. So it is clear that many investors are moving from mutual funds to ETFs. This is particularly true of financial advisors.

Like index mutual funds, most ETFs track a market index, but ETFs offer more index possibilities, including gold and commodities indexes. They also have more transparency than mutual funds as they disclose their holdings every day. In contrast, mutual funds are required to disclose holdings only every six months, or twice a year.

The ETFs also provide more investment options and more pure portfolio hedges. Before the existence of ETFs, an investor who wanted to buy gold as a hedge would probably be forced to & buy a gold mutual fund, which actually invests in mining stocks and other companies that are expected to shine when gold does well. With that kind of fund, even if gold soars, you have no guarantee that your fund will follow it. But with the SPDR Gold Shares, you can actually own gold buillon so it gives you a pure play in that precious metal. That has no doubt had an impact on the flood of money going into gold in 2008–2009.

February 2009 was a big month for the gold fund. As is often the case when stocks fall completely out of favor, some investors turned to gold. In late February, the fund exceeded $30 billion in assets, making it the second-largest ETF. The amount of gold held by the fund was over 1,000 metric tons for the first time, according to a *Wall Street Journal* report on March 2, 2009. This ETF, along with SPY, play a role in creating a diversified portfolio.

ETFs can also be sold short and bought on margin. This means that you can do anything with an ETF that you can do with a stock. The ETFs also carry lower annual expenses than even the lowest cost index mutual funds. But you must pay a commission to buy and sell them as you do with a stock. The ETFs are purchased on the stock exchange rather than from a mutual fund company. Nearly all ETFs are passively managed, tracking a wide variety of sectors, countries, or broad-market indexes. A portfolio of ETFs can be created to offer broad investment sector exposure and diversity. Putting such a portfolio together, through, requires both research and monitoring. This is *not* a portfolio for passive investors, or those who wish to spend little time on investing.

24

Target-Date Funds

IF YOU HAVE A 401(K) PLAN, you've probably heard of target-date funds, which held about 40 percent of 401(k) assets in 2009. Perhaps you've heard of them by another name, such as "lifestyle funds." The idea of such a fund is to provide a mix of assets (a diversified portfolio) that will change over the life of the fund, starting out moderately aggressive and then gradually becoming more conservative over the years until it is invested conservatively to preserve capital in the year that the 401(k) plan participant will actually need her money. The funds themselves come in at least three different flavors: conservative, moderate, and aggressive.

The fund provides diversification and an evolving asset mix in an attempt to meet the needs of the plan participant who intends to retire at a specific time. Target-date funds also provide automatic rebalancing of assets and a long-term perspective rather than looking for today's winner, as some advisors and some individual investors are prone to do.

With these funds, a computer program makes the decisions rather than a human. An asset mix might start at 85 percent stocks and then shift to lower-risk investments as the participant gets closer to his retirement date. These funds got a boost from the Pension Protection Act of 2006, because that law approved them as the default option under automatic enrollment.

The performance of the 2010 funds during the market crash of 2008 and 2009 was carefully scrutinized as it provided the first big test for the funds. At the end of 2008, there was $185 billion total in these funds, according to Cerulli Associates; $26 billion was invested in 2010 target-date funds.

At the beginning of 2009, we heard much about how the funds had failed, that they were a bad idea in the first place, were irresponsibly managed, and so on. Critics focused on the 2010 fund because theoretically investors in this fund might want to have their retirement money available in just a year. As a whole, the funds didn't underperform the market in 2008, but the 2010 funds on average lost 24.6 percent, according to Morningstar Mutual Funds, which is hardly justifiable considering these were supposed to be short-term investments.

Ron Surz, principal at Target Date Analytics, says that the target-date funds have betrayed their shareholders. But some fund managers claim that they did not consider 2010 to be the date the money would be removed from the fund; rather, they saw it as the date the fund investor turned sixty-five. For example, John Cammack, head of third-party distribution at T. Rowe Price, mutual fund managers based in Baltimore, says T. Rowe Price spent a lot of time designing its target-date funds. They were designed as if they would manage a portfolio twenty or thirty years into retirement rather than to see the target date as the stop date. So the allocation is just about evenly split between stocks and bonds at retirement date. And stocks continue to make up 26 percent of the T. Rowe Price portfolio of a ninety-year-old who retired at age sixty-five, Cammack says.

Surz dismisses all this talk about managing mortality risk as nothing more than a smoke screen. The truth, he says, is that "the target-date industry entered into a performance race in 2007, raising equity allocations and justifying the increase as necessitated by longer life expectancies." Surz sees no reason to expect a target-date fund to last beyond the target date. Not that he expects the money to disappear; instead, he expects the retiree to make a decision about her savings at retirement. Surz also points out his indexes, which have been branded the "On Target Index" by *Plan Sponsor* magazine, are the most conservative, particularly near the target date, and that they diversify across the globe rather than just in the United States.

So what should 401(k) plan participants know about these funds? For one thing, they should realize that there is no formula that holds constant. Funds with the same 2010 target date varied from 21 percent in equities to 90 percent in equities.

The biggest retirement debate swings around the problem of outliving your assets. Managers who believe that outliving your assets is the biggest risk to retirees tend to put more assets into equity because they say that the return on equities will outdistance inflation.

Surz argues that this is only a smokescreen, they put more money into equity to chase performance. I think the funds are still a better default option than a money fund. But clearly they have limitations. Should you choose one? You should not choose one and then forget about it, believing that your retirement is safe and that the fund gives you a guarantee. It does not. There are no "buy and forget" investments.

Expenses

IF THERE IS A CATCH TO 401(κ) PLANS, it is this: they cost too much. When the plans were introduced more than twenty-five years ago, the employer typically paid the plan's fees. Remember that employers were eager to encourage their employees to set aside money for their retirement. Also, the early plans were not as expensive as they have become today.

There are three basic cost components to a 401(k) plan:

■ **Investment management costs.** The cost of managing the money in the plan, which is expressed as a percent of assets.

■ **Trustee costs.** Costs that can be separated into custody charges and general processing fees. Services in this category—such as cutting a check for a loan—can be charged per activity. In that way, the person who uses the service pays the fee rather than making it an implicit cost of the plan.

■ **Administration costs.** Includes record keeping and employee communication and education, as well as many of the fancy frills.

When a 401(k) plan uses mutual funds, many of these fees are wrapped into the mutual fund expense ratio and paid by the mutual fund investors. That is money that is subtracted from mutual fund assets each year. It is expressed as a percent of assets, usually in basis points. A basis point is 1/100th of one percent. So if the annual expense ratio is 1 percent, it might be expressed as 100 basis points. An expense ratio of 0.25 percent is expressed as 25 basis points.

Many 401(k) plans use open-end mutual funds that are also available to regular retail investors who buy the funds outside of a 401(k) plan. When that's the case, who subsidizes whom? Does the retail investor subsidize the 401(k) plan participant or vice versa? I've made the argument that the retail investors subsidize the 401(k) plan investors, because retirement plans have added many bells and whistles resulting in increased fees. Plan sponsors also sometimes add additional administrative expenses to the 401(k) fees. And most employers have passed the fees on to plan participants. In a long bull market, high fees are more tolerable as returns are higher, too. But in the market of 2008 and 2009, when many investors have lost big chunks of the money in their plans, they are not willing to pay what they may consider excessive fees.

At the end of February 2009, for example, mutual funds held $5.9 trillion, down from $8 trillion at the start of 2008, according to Morningstar. Because the fund expense ratio is computed by dividing total fees by assets, fees are increasing just as fund assets are decreasing. In March 2009, Vanguard, long touted as the low fee provider of mutual funds, announced that it would raise fees. Vanguard will still be the low fee provider. In 2008, the average expense ratio on a Vanguard fund was 0.2 percent or 20 basis points. The average increase on a Vanguard fund is 0.05 percent or 5 basis points, while the average fee for a U.S. stock fund in 2008 was 1.6 percent, according to Morningstar Mutual Funds. For an international stock fund, the average was 1.8 percent, and for a taxable bond fund, 1.3 percent, according to Morningstar.

Many fund companies also charge 12B-1 fees, a separate annual charge that comes out of the fund assets. This fee is authorized by the Securities and Exchange Commission (SEC) to pay for marketing and distribution costs. Sometimes a 401(k) plan will add this extra fee to pay a consultant who puts together an alliance or group of funds to be offered in 401(k) plans. Then current participants are forced to pay so the fund can get into other markets.

Reject 12B-1 fees. Some small-company plans use mutual funds with loads or commissions, and they may add yet another layer of annual fees that are charge based on a percent of assets in the plan. If you are offered a plan where the employer contributes nothing in the way of a match, and you are losing 2 to 3 percent of your contribution each year to a combination of commission and fees, complain. And then explore other options.

Get the Prospectus

YOUR EMPLOYER IS NOT LEGALLY required to provide you with the prospectus for mutual funds offered in your 401(k) plan. That's because the 401(k) trust is the legal owner of the mutual fund shares, not the 401(k) plan participant. So the mutual fund company must provide the trust with the prospectus for each fund. The trust doesn't have to pass the prospectus on, yet most employers do.

If yours is one that does pass along the prospectus, take a look at it. If not, get a copy for yourself or, better yet, go to the fund's Web site. If your plan's mutual funds are sponsored by one of the retail mutual fund companies like American, Fidelity, Vanguard, or T. Rowe Price, you can get a copy by calling the company and asking for one or downloading it.

A mutual fund prospectus can make for dull reading. But it's worth your effort to find out the fund's objectives, restrictions on the portfolio manager, fees, and other charges. Pay special attention to the following items:

Summary of expenses. Look here for the annual fund operating expenses, the cost of running the fund. These include the management fee, which covers salaries and administrative expenses and the 12B-1 fee, which covers marketing expenses. Most funds also have a category called "other expenses," which includes miscellaneous fees.

In 1980, the average fee for a stock mutual fund was 2.32 percent, according to the Investment Company Institute (ICI), the industry association. In 2008, the average fee for a U.S. stock fund was 1.6 percent, according to Morningstar Mutual Funds, and a bit lower based on ICI figures.

Look, too, at the example, which the company is required to provide, of what you would pay on a $1,000 investment assuming a 5 percent annual return and redemption at the end of the time period.

Financial history. This history shows up to ten years of the fund's performance. Check to see if the fund has cut into net asset value (NAV) to pay out dividends. Is the expense ratio declining over time or increasing? Is the portfolio turnover rate fairly steady and modest, for example, in the 50 percent range?

Investment objective. This states where the manager will put most of her money. For example, "The fund will invest substantially all of its assets—but no less than 80 percent—in common stocks."

Performance. Look at the fund's total return for the past ten years, which is calculated according to Securities and Exchange Commission (SEC) regulations. It will be compared with an index, usually the S&P index for a domestic stock fund. Don't expect your fund to beat the index every year. That's unrealistic. The only way it could do that is if it took on much more risk than the index. Instead, look for consistency. Check to see how the fund did in years when the S&P was down as well as the S&P's best years. You want a smooth ride.

I looked on the Vanguard Web site to get information on a fund I have in my retirement account called Vanguard Health Care. Here are some of the things I learned: The fund seeks to provide long-term capital appreciation by investing in U.S. and foreign stocks related to health care. The expense ratio is 26 basis points. The fund charges a 1 percent redemption fee on shares held less than one year to discourage short-term trading.

I was aware of the 1 percent redemption fee, which doesn't affect me as I've held the fund for years. However, I did not realize the fund imposed a minimum investment of $25,000. That was not true when I bought it for my Individual Retirement Account (IRA) or for my kids' college accounts. That means I must weigh carefully whether to sell this fund because I will not be able to get back in unless I have $25,000 to invest. I also found information on the Web site about which stocks the fund holds, the fund's management, and other performance details. Check your own investments once a year to make certain you understand the fund or account you use.

Rebalance

ONCE YOU'VE THOUGHT through your risk tolerance, looked at asset classes, made your investment selections, and started your 401(k) plan contributions, are you finished? Not quite. Now you must do two things that are seemingly contradictory. First, you must have the discipline to stick with your plan. Second, you must rebalance your investments once a year.

One of the keys to investment success is to avoid second-guessing yourself and to stick with the asset allocation you've made no matter what happens in the markets. So when you read that the stock market is getting too high, just let that information roll by.

However, your asset allocation will grow out of balance simply because of the cycles in the investment markets. That's when you should do something. Think of it as weeding a garden. You've selected the plants well, now you must control their growth. For many investors, that's the toughest part. That was particularly difficult at the end of 2008 because it meant putting more money into stocks, which had suffered so drastically in 2008. And the trouble was, stocks started off 2009 by doing even worse. Most investors were terrified that the market and life as we know it were over. Many of them decided to sell their stocks rather than buying more to rebalance their portfolios. Can you blame them? If the stocks in your portfolio are down by half, it takes great discipline to keep adding stocks. But that's exactly what you should do.

Consider this simplistic example. Suppose you have 50 percent in an S&P index fund, 25 percent in a small-cap fund and 25 percent in an international fund. If the international fund takes off, and your investment doubles while U.S. stocks remain flat, perhaps you have 50 percent in international, 20 percent in the S&P index, and 30 percent in small-company funds because they did better than the large-company funds in the S&P index.

I realize this example might seem foolish to investors today when all market segments cratered in 2008. Yet some sectors of the market do better than others and disciplining yourself to sell off a winner can be tough. For example, investing in Asia (minus Japan) was a good choice in late 2002. It could be done by buying an exchange-traded fund (ETF) called iShares MSCI Pacific ex-Japan index fund (EPP). This fund split 3 for 1 in July 2008 because it had outperformed the market and the net asset value (NAV) had gotten so high. Of course it's tempting to stick with your winners. But no sector of the market will outperform indefinitely. It is the emotional attachment to investments that trips up most investors. If you understand market cycles, you know that what goes up comes down. The East Asia area around Japan that was developing and growing at a much faster pace than Europe and the U.S. got caught up in the market chaos that enveloped the world in late 2008 and began to sink.

Rebalancing—if it is done rigorously and unemotionally—helps you to do what all investors should: buy low and sell high. It encourages making contrarian plays because you are selling the investments that have done well and buying those that have done poorly. In our example, the U.S. stocks will have their run-ups too. If you rebalance, you will catch them before they start to move. For example, consider SPY, an ETF that invests in the S&P's 500, or the overall market for big-cap stocks. In early March 2009, when the world economy looked dreadful, SPY hit a low of 67.10. But on September 18, 2009, SPY closed at 106.72.

Rebalancing need not be complex. It can be done with only two funds if necessary. Suppose you have a stock index fund and a guaranteed investment contract, or GIC, which offers a guaranteed return. You might put 75 percent in the stock fund and 25 percent in the GIC and rebalance once a year so that you add to stocks when the market is down and sell off your gains when the market is up.

One of the problems I see for 401(k) plan participants going forward from 2009 is that they will be so fearful of the stock market that they will demand guaranteed investments. Because of the growing budget deficit in the United States, inflation promises to be a bigger problem going forward. Some experts believe we will see a replay of the 1970s when inflation between January 1971 and December 1978 totaled 71.61 percent.

We can't make predictions on inflation. But the key to rebalancing is to remove all emotion from it. Don't try to guess when it's time to sell one fund and buy another or to redirect your investments. That amounts to trying to time the market, which cannot be done successfully. Instead, pick a date, perhaps the first day of the year, and ruthlessly sell off the winners and add to the losers. Your 401(k) plan is the perfect place to do this because there are no tax consequences when you sell.

What Not to Buy

THERE ARE SOME INVESTMENTS that do not belong in your retirement plan. Chief among them is stock in your employer's company, insurance products, and municipal bonds.

Many companies offer company stock as one of their 401(k) plan options. Do not choose it. You already have your livelihood tied up with your employer, who pays your salary and offers you employee benefits such as health care and holiday and vacation pay. You do not want to have your retirement savings tied to the fate of the same company.

If your portfolio's value rests on a single stock, you risk financial disaster if the company runs into trouble. The first "shock" in this regard came in the early to mid-1990s when IBM stock was golden and the company prided itself on never laying off an employee. Then thousands of employees were forced out of Big Blue at the same time that the company's stock hit the skids. But this was a mild example compared to what was to come.

Remember what happened to Enron employees who invested most or all of their 401(k) money in Enron stock? Ten years ago, Enron was touted as the company of the future. Unfortunately, I was an investor in Enron when the stock plunged from $90 a share in August 2000 to less than $1 a share in November 2001. Sure it hurt my portfolio. A big chunk of it simply disappeared. But thousands of Enron employees were wiped out. And we have many more recent examples of companies like Lehman Brothers, American International Group (AIG), Citibank, General Motors (GM), and Chrysler where employees who own stock in the company they work for have been devastated.

Some companies offer only company stock as their match for the 401(k) plan. And, of course, many companies see it as a mark of employee loyalty to choose company stock to show your faith in the company. You can't afford to do that though. Look what happened to employees at the companies I've just mentioned. Many of them were wiped out. Experts say you should never have more than 10 percent of your portfolio in one company's stock and that your own company stock should represent much less. I think 10 percent in any one stock is too much for your 401(k) plan. And 1 percent in your employer's stock is too much. Bottom line: If employer stock is the only option, contribute enough to get the employer match and shift the money out as soon as possible.

Tax-advantaged investments like municipal bonds and life insurance products are not good retirement account vehicles either. Financing a retirement plan with pre-tax dollars is a big advantage for investors, who do not have to pay taxes until they make withdrawals. But buying a tax-advantaged investment within the plan provides no extra tax benefit. In this category are municipal bonds, whose income is free from federal income taxes, and life insurance policies, whose cash value grows tax deferred. Of course, the decision is more difficult if you have no choice. For example, participants in 403(b) plans may find that an annuity is their only option. In that case, weigh other factors such as the convenience of payroll deduction to invest for retirement and an employer match if there is one and the attractiveness of the investments. But pay careful attention to fees and expenses.

Insurers frequently urge people to buy a life insurance policy, or an annuity, inside a retirement plan, arguing that premiums can be paid with pretax money. True. But Glenn Daily, a fee-only insurance consultant in New York, calls that advice misguided. "A retirement plan is the only way to buy mutual funds with tax-deductible dollars," he says, "and the return is a lot better [than on a life insurance policy]."

High fees are a drag on insurance returns, too. In a report for a city whose employees bought life insurance in a retirement plan, Ethan E. Kra, chief actuary at Mercer management consultants, found that 100 percent of the first-year premiums went to sales costs and none went to investments.

An annuity is an insurance company product that offers tax-deferred buildup of earnings. Like insurance policies and municipal bonds, annuities have no place in retirement accounts. Fees on these products are high to provide for the life insurance guarantees that are wrapped into them but do not add value to the investment. Most retirement plans have a choice of investments. When you have a choice, keep it simple. Go for the low-cost, no-frills basic mutual funds or ETFs. Avoid your company's stock, municipal bonds, and insurance company products.

PART FIVE

PREPARING FOR CHANGE

The Next Step

Planning and saving well in advance make the transition to retirement much smoother. But it is how you handle the transition from a full-time employer that sponsors your 401(k) plan to the next phase of your life that will make the biggest difference in your satisfaction and happiness.

Perhaps that step leads to retirement. More likely though, you will be exchanging one kind of work for another. Please don't think that sounds dreary. Work is one of only a handful of essentials to a happy life—along with food, shelter, and love.

It's never too late to pursue your dreams through work. Brendan Gill, a former staff writer for the *New Yorker*, picked seventy-five famous and not-so-famous late bloomers, like Grandma Moses, for his book of portraits by the same name (*Late Bloomers*, Artisan 1998). "If the hour happens to be later than we may have wished, take heart!" Gill wrote. "So much more to be cherished is the bloom."

Over the last decade, more and more people continue to work past retirement. And to answer the needs of baby boomer retirees to keep a hand in, a number of "temporary employment" centers have opened to allow part-time retirees to continue to work on a project basis.

So what will you do in your post-corporate life? Make room for passion and for surprise. Perhaps you will turn a long-time hobby into a part-time business. Maybe build a second career. Your work need not be paid to be satisfying, of course. Do you hope to spend the bulk of your time with a theater or church group, building houses for Habitat for Humanity, scuba diving, studying Italian, or raising horses? I have friends who joined the Peace Corps when they retired.

Whatever you do, it will require careful planning—both financial and lifestyle planning. But don't think too narrowly about it. Remember

George Kinder, the life planning guru in the introduction? Kinder argues that a good life and a good retirement require passion. Several of the financial planners he has trained in his workshops developed their own passions and rebuilt their lives around them.

Consider Marjorie A. Burnett, a financial advisor who has been through Kinder's workshops to become a registered life planner. In 2008, I spent a few days with Burnett while I attended a Kinder workshop in Arlington, Virginia. Burnett worked in various fields and locations around the world before deciding to leave the corporate world and explore her next career. Like many baby boomers at midlife, she wanted a job that would give her the satisfaction of knowing that her work was helping her clients lead more satisfying lives. She wanted to do something both grounded and spiritual and to develop in her own life at the same time. Burnett, who wears a long braid to her waist, eschews makeup, and dresses neatly but casually, is exactly the type of planner I would choose because she has given so much thought to her own life and is a great listener.

Burnett, who has a law degree and is a certified public accountant, worked as a CPA tax consultant for fifteen years, primarily at KPMG, then went to law school full time for three years, clerked in federal district court for two years and worked as a corporate tax attorney at Miller & Chevalier for six years. When her mother died in 2001, she says, "I paused and realized how important it was to me to feel that my work makes a positive difference in the world." She needed "greater meaning in my work and I wanted a different lifestyle." She'd always been interested in personal finance, she liked problem solving, and she saw that her background would fit well with financial planning. "I dove into the CFP [certified financial planner] coursework and passed the exam in 2004."

But as she set up her office as a solo practitioner, she realized that financial planning required more than business, marketing, and regulatory compliance. "It also entails working with clients in such a way that they are motivated to take steps to achieve their financial goals." So she began taking courses on entrepreneurship at the same time she adjusted to working from home rather than in a large law office with an assistant, computer support, and a strong research library. In order to succeed, Burnett realized she needed to do some work on her self;

she continued a yoga program and the Alexander Technique lessons she began several years ago and looked for new growth opportunities.

The Alexander Technique was developed by F. M. Alexander (1869–1955) a Shakespearean actor who discovered that his own movement was responsible for his chronic hoarseness. He researched and studied human movement, solved his problem and began to teach others how to balance their bodies and cure pain and discomfort (http://www.alexandertech.org/misc/whatisat.html). The technique involves a series of lessons with a practitioner. In September 2009, Burnett was considering going to New York to study to become a practitioner, which takes several years.

Countless people have followed a path similar to Burnett's to find that their happiest and most satisfying career experiences came when they were most themselves and helping clients to follow that path as well. Some of them, like Susan Crandell, former editor at *Ladies Home Journal* and founding editor of *MORE*, a magazine for women over forty, left her lifetime career in the magazine business to write a book, *Thinking about Tomorrow: Reinventing Yourself at Midlife*, about how transitions at midlife or later provide Americans with a joyous second act.

Crandell offers some interesting stories and resources in her book. There are also many Web resources for people who want to find new work, project work, or part-time work at midlife, such as www.retiredbrains.com. Another site, www.coolworks.com, cites jobs in exotic places such as Alaska or Mesa Verde, a park in Colorado that holds the spectacular cliff dwellings and mesa top pueblo sites. Here we will provide information on how to best plan and make your own transition to retirement.

Get Real

FINANCIAL PLANNERS say that clients often approach them at age fifty, fifty-five, or even sixty-five and ask if they can retire, even though they have just $10,000 or so in the bank and no pension or other retirement income. Of course, financial planners use all kinds of tools to project how much you'll need in retirement and how much your current nest egg can be expected to grow. Hint: $10,000 will not get you too far into your first year.

But we shouldn't be surprised that Americans have an unrealistic view of retirement. Haven't we been told that retirement is the pot of gold at the end of the rainbow? Shouldn't we expect to be rewarded after a lifetime of hard work? Americans simply want a piece of that good life they keep reading about. The financial crisis of 2008–09 has punctured some of those unrealistic ideas.

Still, I blame the personal finance magazines like *Money* for stoking that dream, especially in the 1990s when the stock market was blowing its tech bubble until it burst in 2000. I include myself as part of that problem. Investment advice was hot news. Doubling your money in stocks gave you bragging rights at the cocktail parties or bridge clubs or book clubs or jazz clubs or wherever you hung out.

Everybody wanted to talk about the market—all the better if the news could show you how to retire in your fifties and live the good life. The end of the last century was an extremely difficult time for financial advisors who refused to go with the flow and buy high-tech for client portfolios. Many of these advisors stubbornly refused to give up on their asset allocations and put everything in high-tech. Some told me that they lost clients because of it. Who wanted a diversified portfolio when all the returns were coming from technology and other growth stocks?

At industry conferences I attended, speakers argued that the Cold War was over, only peace and prosperity and bull markets lay ahead—or at least, that's how it seemed, until 2000 when the tech bubble burst. But Americans still kept spending, driving the savings rate into negative territory in 2005, according to the U.S. Commerce

Department: indeed, 2005 was only the third year our economy showed a negative savings rate, the others being 1932 and 1933.

Did the financial collapse at the end of 2008, when home values plummeted and stock portfolios nearly disappeared, shatter the last of those unrealistic dreams and give baby boomers, and their children and grandchildren, a dose of reality? Americans began to pay off debts, curb spending, and start saving, bringing the U.S. savings rate up to 5.7 percent in April 2009. The market collapse sowed a lot of pain, but perhaps it also helped us focus on the truth: Thirty years of traveling the world by boat and eating exotic food is not a realistic idea of retirement.

A closer look at some of those inspiring stories shows that if we had paid closer attention to the numbers, we would have realized how unrealistic the goals were. Consider the cover story in the April 1997 issue of *Money* magazine. A young, single music teacher; a divorcing dad; a couple with young kids; another who owns a business—all will retire with more than a million dollars and no sweat in getting there, according to the article. But take a closer look and you'll see that the divorcing dad must invest $9,500, the maximum for that year, in his 403(b) retirement plan as well as "sock away" $2,400 a month in his stock portfolio to reach his goal. That's $28,800 after taxes in addition to the $9,500 in the retirement plan. Few of us were "socking away" that much in 1997, and even fewer of us can manage it in 2009. And few of us will retire at age fifty or fifty-five.

So instead of focusing on when you can drop the "ball-and-chain" and head to the Florida Keys in your sailboat, get real. Think about leaving your job as a transition and focus on what you really want to do when you switch gears.

Money should not be your only consideration. If you've had a high-powered career, and you've been working hard for thirty years, lying on the beach may sound appealing, but the reality of it probably won't satisfy the person you have become. Changing the structure of your life requires a lot of thought. It's difficult to simply imagine how you will feel in an entirely, new situation. Try to test it out. When my husband and I decided to leave New York City and move to the Hudson Valley, we spent a summer house sitting for friends on long Island to see if the move might be a terrible mistake. For us, it wasn't.

Thinking about Tomorrow

ADAPTING TO A MAJOR LIFE transition requires considerable gear shifting as well as some financial reserves, courage, and a sense of adventure. When Susan Crandell walked away from her dream job as editor-in-chief of *MORE* magazine to become a freelance writer, she wondered if she would really find the better life she sought, if her life would ever again be as interesting as it had been as founding editor of a magazine whose circulation climbed to 1 million in six years, thanks to the stories of exciting adventures and decisions that women made in their forties, fifties, and sixties. The magazine was successful because many women at midlife wanted to gain inspiration to make tough decisions themselves. Susan is a business source I wrote stories for when she was editor of *Ladies Home Journal* and later when she was editor at *MORE*. We've also ridden several Century Rides together. The Century is a 100 mile ride; the one we do takes place in the Hudson Valley at leaf turning times.

A *MORE* survey found that nearly three quarters of the upscale, educated readership of the magazine weren't crazy about their jobs. Crandell had always been an adventurer—bungee jumping with her daughter in New Zealand—but considered herself risk averse when it came to needing a regular salary. So she wanted some extra inspiration herself. Combining her newfound freedom with the knowledge that she wasn't the only middle-aged person thinking about changing her life, she set off to investigate what she calls "life entrepreneurs": people who act on their vision of a "richer, fuller" future for themselves at mid-life or later.

The result was *Thinking About Tomorrow*, a look at forty-five people who reinvented themselves at midlife and the lessons they learned along the way. These people weren't only career changers: their transformations encompass spirituality, education, gender, and many alternative approaches to the world. In turn, Crandell learned a lot about what goes into a successful midlife makeover.

In the book, Crandell says the old midlife crisis—buying a sports car, having an affair, and then realizing that it doesn't provide the right answer—is over. And so is accepting the fact that the best part of your life is in the past. The baby boomer at midlife "sees the yearnings and dissatisfaction of midlife as a call to action rather than a curse. Midlife crisis becomes midlife opportunity," Crandell writes. And the people in her book jump at the opportunity: to become first-time parents, to climb mountains, go heli-skiing and start new careers in foreign places. In an interview with Lifetwo.com, a Web site about midlife improvement, Crandell was asked if anything about her new life surprised her.

"What's surprised not just me, but my family, is that it has actually changed my personality," she said. "When I ran *MORE*, I was a woman with a plan. My entire week was carefully cho-reographed, with no room for slippage. Now, I'm more relaxed, more contemplative. I was describing this to a newspaper reporter the other day, and when I put down the phone, I asked my daughter whether it was really true. 'Absolutely,' she said. And 'Hallelujah.'"

Lifetwo.com is a good source for information about midlife as well. According to the site, visitors in 2008 came from 210 countries, with about 70 percent from the United States. The largest audience is in New York City, followed by London and Sydney. Most visitors found the site by searching Google for keywords such as "midlife crisis."

Magazines like *MORE* and books and Web sites about resources for mid life tensional are abundant today. Many of them are inspiring as well as useful.

Pay Off Debt

AMERICANS AT ALL STAGES of life carry too much debt. As you prepare for retirement, paying off debt should be a top financial priority for two reasons. First, there's nowhere else you can get a guaranteed investment return equal to what you get by investing in your debt. Paying it off yields a risk-free return of whatever your interest rate happens to be. Paying off $2,500 at 16 percent yields a 16 percent return on that money. Second, it will give you flexibility by freeing up your cash flow so that you may be able to do something creative during the next phase of your life.

Here's a plan to help you become debt-free:

1. **Figure out how much you owe.** Gather all your credit card statements and make a list that includes the interest rate, total balance and minimum monthly payment. List the highest-rate card first and so on. "A lot of people lose track of what they owe," says Gerri Detweiler, one of the country's top credit specialists, who serves as a credit advisor for Credit.com, a free Web site offering a wealth of tools to help consumers improve their financial lives.

2. **Keep the two cards with the lowest rates.** Cut the others up. Write to the card issuers and ask that those accounts be closed.

3. **If you do not have a card with an interest rate below 14 percent, get one.** CardTrak.com offers screens for credit cards depending on what you are looking for: the lowest rate, frequent flyer miles, discount merchandise.

4. **Resolve that you will use your cards only for essentials over the next six months.** For other purchases, use cash or a debit card. A debit card, which taps into your bank account when you make purchases, provides good discipline. If you don't have the money, you can't spend it.

5. **Add up your minimum monthly payments.** Credit cards often require very low minimums. Follow them and you will be paying

forever. For instance, if you owe $1,000 on a card with 17 percent interest rate, it might take you twelve years and cost you $979 to pay it off if you make only the minimum payment.

6. Calculate how much you can pay in addition to the minimum. Really stretch here. For instance, let's suppose the minimum payments on your credit cards total $350 a month. What could you pay if you really pushed it? How about $750? No pain, no gain.

7. Apply all of your additional repayment to the card with the highest rate. If two cards have the same rate, put the additional money on the card with the largest balance. This makes the most effective use of your money because it saves the most in interest.

8. Consolidate your debt. Many credit card issuers offer introductory rates as low as 5.9 percent or 6.9 percent—or sometimes even zero—for six months. If you are really serious about getting out of debt in a hurry, transfer your largest, high-rate balances to a card with an extremely low rate and pay them off aggressively. Monitor the rates carefully. When the rate goes up, shift to another card if the rate is high and you have not managed to pay off the debt.

9. Pay the minimum on your lowest-rate cards until you've paid off the balance on the more expensive cards.

10. Consider using your savings to get out of debt. Harsh! I agree. But if you put together a balance sheet, your debt would cancel your savings anyhow. If those savings are in the bank, you're earning around 1 percent to carry debt at 18 percent.

In the spring of 2009, credit card issuers got very aggressive about raising credit card rates and fee. Some have doubled interest rates as well as minimum payments. Do your best to get out of this stranglehold.

Besides offering information about credit at Credit.com, Gerri Detweiler co-authored *Debt Collection Answers,* an e-book that can be downloaded on your computer as well as *Reduce Debt, Reduce Stress* (Good Advice Press, 2009).

Your Mortgage

PAYING OFF CREDIT CARD debt is a no-brainer, but what about other kinds of debt? How should you weigh paying down debt vs. tucking extra money away? Although car loans generally carry lower interest rates than credit cards, they, too, should be paid down to prepare for the time you will be living on a lower income. Interest on these loans is not tax deductible, so you carry the full cost of it.

Paying off mortgage debt is more controversial. Many investors have argued that they can get a better return on their money by investing in the stock market rather than in their own mortgage, especially if they carry a low interest rate such as 5 percent on a fixed-rate loan. Yet most financial advisors suggest that clients pay off their home before they leave their jobs.

Paying off the mortgage isn't a new idea. It has its roots in the debt aversion fostered in the Great Depression. Many Americans who went through the Depression vowed they would never owe money again. But the debt free movement also has a modern missionary in Marc Eisenson, author of *The Banker's Secret.* In the book, Eisenson argues that by prepaying you are actually "investing in your mortgage," earning a return of whatever your interest rate happens to be.

Eisenson's book, which is composed chiefly of tables illustrating the effect of prepayments, shows, for example, that a homeowner who shells out an additional $200 a month shaves $153,414 in interest and six years off a $350,000, 30 year mortgage at 8 percent. The same $200 trims 11½ years off a $150,000 loan with similar terms.

Eisenson's case for prepayment is a powerful one. But savvy investors found it too simplistic. They argued that when you prepay a mortgage, you lose not only the tax deduction on the interest rate but also the opportunity to invest the funds elsewhere for a higher return. That made the idea workable only for those who didn't itemize or those in lower tax brackets. Those with big bucks and big taxes were better off with the deduction. But many tax and savings rules of thumb, like this one, are no longer operative.

First, a tax change in 1990 reduced the dollar amount of most itemized deductions, including home mortgage interest, for those in upper tax brackets. These taxpayers must subtract a portion of their adjusted gross income from their itemized deductions, making the mortgage interest deduction worth less. In 2009, the Obama administration has talked about further limits on tax deductions for those above certain income levels.

I often interviewed Eisenson when I lived in Manhattan. When I moved to the Hudson Valley, I discovered he did, too. I once went to lunch with him and Nancy Castleman and discovered two people who walk their talk, growing their own food, living simply and encouraging others to do so as well through the publication of their goodadvicepress.com. I recommend their book *Invest in Yourself.*

For these and other reasons, financial planners give serious thought to paying off the mortgage for clients at all stages of life. But for those nearing retirement, it's a slam dunk, for psychological reasons as well as economic reasons. Most people simply feel better knowing they own their home free and clear. "We don't make decisions for purely financial reasons," says Judith Shine, a planner in Denver, Colorado. "We make decisions that help people live a happier life."

Of course, you can hardly expect to pay off a lump sum of $100,000 in this housing market when many homeowners cannot even keep up with mortgage payments. The real estate Web site www .Zillow.com has reported that 21.8 percent of all U.S. homes, representing more than 21 million residences, were in a "negative equity" or "underwater" position after prices dropped more than 14 percent nationally in the year ended March 31, 2009. "In some markets, more than half of all homes are in negative equity," according to the Web site.

Many of us will feel lucky just making our regular mortgage payments. But if you have any extra dollars, putting them into your mortgage is a great way of saving money and becoming more financially secure.

5

Paperwork Matters

BEING ORGANIZED is important at all stages of your financial life. Yet most of us never get around to it and we still manage to muddle through. When you're headed for a big life transition, though, order is essential.

Now you will need records that show how much you paid for your home and the cost of improvements you've made. You may need copies of your cash-value insurance policies, which can serve as a source of income in retirement. You'll need your birth certificate to apply for Social Security. And you must have pension records, investment records for stocks, bond and mutual funds, and records that show contributions and withdrawals from retirement accounts.

You also need to pull together some financial statements for your personal business. That means figuring out your net worth and then seeing what you might do to spruce it up a bit as well as drawing up an income statement or a budget that shows what's coming in and what's going out.

Start by pulling together these things:

■ **A copy of your most recent income tax return.**

■ **Records of liquid assets.** You need to know exactly how much you have in checking and savings accounts, bank certificates of deposit, and money market accounts.

■ **Copies of life insurance policies with records of accumulated cash values.** You should receive an annual statement from the insurer that shows current cash value as well as the current death benefit. On many policies, the death benefit increases as the policy generates what are called "paid up additions," or tiny little policies that are added to the big one. You'll want to know the current death benefit as well as your ability to generate tax-free income from your cash value. You can do this by taking tax-free loans from the policy, which need never be paid back provided you keep the policy in force. You need good advice on this strategy, so do some research to find it.

■ **Annual statement from your employer that shows the value of your pension plan, 401(k) plan, and any other tax-deferred savings.**

■ **A benefits statement that shows the value of life insurance and other employer benefits, as well as retiree medical benefits, if any.**

■ **Statements for individual retirement accounts (IRAs) and other retirement accounts for the self-employed.**

■ **Records of investment assets including stocks, bonds, mutual funds, investment real estate, and limited partnerships.**

■ **Information about real estate holdings.** If you own a home or apartment, figure out what you owe on your mortgage and what the home is worth. Ditto for a vacation home. Get information, too, on your car(s) or other vehicles you own.

■ **An estimate of the value of collectibles, including coins, antiques, art or anything else of value.** Be realistic about the value of things like your comic book collection.

■ **Records for valuable jewelry, furs, or hand-tied Oriental rugs.** As a practical matter, your personal belongings, like the clothes you wear to work and the couch in the living room, don't add much to your net worth. But if you own some valuable stuff, you'll want to list it as an asset. Include computer equipment.

■ **Records of your debts including copies of a couple of recent credit card statements.** Also pull out payment books for your car and for any other personal loans, installment loans, and home equity loans.

■ **Records that show the value of your business, if you are self-employed.**

■ **Records of business receivables.**

How to Organize It

ACCOUNTANTS SAY THAT PEOPLE make two kinds of mistakes when it comes to keeping records. The first is to keep everything— expired refrigerator warranties, receipts from the doughnut shop, last year's income tax return—in one jumbled box. The second is to throw everything out.

If you fall into either one of these groups, there's still hope for you. Like most other financial tasks, record keeping is not difficult. Boring? Maybe. At the beginning it may be time consuming but once you get your files set up, maintenance is fairly simple.

Label six folders as follows:

■ **Personal,** which includes all family records, such as birth and marriage papers, adoption and custody papers, university diplomas, military papers, membership certificates, licenses, and wills;

■ **Property,** which includes documents like deeds, receipts, and appraisals;

■ **Financial,** which includes investments, IRAs, 401(k) accounts, loan papers, credit card records, bank accounts, trust agreements, and mutual fund statements;

■ **Insurance,** for your policies and claim settlement records and receipts;

■ **Tax**;

■ **Medical,** for health records and prescriptions, statements from hospitals, reports of medical exams.

Here are some rules of thumb on what to keep:

■ **Personal records** that document birth, marriage, and divorce should be kept forever. Other records that should be kept indefinitely include military papers, medical records, wills, and trust agreements.

■ **Investment documents,** such as brokerage and mutual fund statements, and stock option agreements should be kept in your "keep forever" files.

■ **Records on property you inherit** should also be kept. Your "cost basis," or the cost on which your capital gains tax will be calculated, is determined by the property's market value when you inherited it. Those without records may be forced to pay capital gains on the entire sales price.

■ You should also keep retirement plan agreements, insurance policies, wills, trust agreements, and powers of attorney.

■ **Tax documents** should be kept for at least ten years, if not longer. The Internal Revenue Service (IRS) has three years from the time of filing to assess additional taxes. For that reason, many people believe they need to keep tax records for only three years. But the statue of limitations stretches to six years if a taxpayer omits income exceeding 25 percent of the income reported. And there is no statue of limitations on returns where the IRS finds fraud.

■ Keep with your tax records those records of property that has a "cost basis" for tax purposes. These include records that document what you paid for your home and the money you laid out for improvements. These records must be kept until you sell the property so that you can establish your basis for capital gains purposes.

■ **Consumer records** such as receipts, invoices, and warranties need be kept only as long as you own the property. While you're getting organized, though, make a list of credit cards with phone numbers so that you can call the company in the event they are stolen. List, too, your financial representatives, including your accountant, insurance agent, financial planner, or stockbroker with phone numbers. Keep this list with your financial records.

What's Your Net Worth?

YOU NEED A BALANCE SHEET to show what you own and what you owe as well as the decisions you've made about spending your money over the years. It should be divided into two broad categories: assets, or what you have, and liabilities, or what you owe. The assets category is subdivided into three smaller categories: liquid, investment, and personal assets.

Net-Worth Statement

Liquid assets

Cash (checking, savings accounts)	$_____
Certificates of deposit	$_____
Money market funds	$_____
Other	$_____
Total liquid assets	$_____

Investment assets

Stock	$_____
Bonds	$_____
Mutual funds	$_____
Life insurance cash values	$_____
Investment real estate	$_____
Limited partnerships	$_____
Collectibles	$_____
Precious metals	$_____
Other	$_____
Total Investment assets	$_____

Personal assets

Personal residence	$_____
Vacation home	$_____
Automobiles	$_____

Household furnishings/rugs/art $_____
Clothing/jewelry $_____
Computer equipment $_____
Total personal assets $_____

TOTAL ASSETS $_____
Now list everything you owe:

Short-term debt
MasterCard/Visa/Discover/
  American Express $_____
Bank overdraft line $_____
Home equity loans $_____
Student/business loans $_____
Car/equipment loans $_____
Other debt $_____
Total short-term debt $_____

Long-term debt
Home mortgage $_____
Mortgage on second home $_____
Other long-term debt $_____
Total long-term debt $_____
TOTAL DEBT $_____

Now subtract your liabilities—or debt—from your assets. That's your net worth. Look at how your wealth is spread among the three asset classes. To be prepared for emergencies, you need three months' worth of living expenses in liquid assets. If you are approaching retirement, you should increase your cash to three years of living expenses.

If your balance sheet shows that most of your assets are in the personal category, think about changing the way you deploy your money. You should aim to increase your net worth each year—by paying down debt, paying off your mortgage, pumping more money into your 401(k) account and other investments.

Your Financial Statement

TO FIGURE OUT what you'll need in retirement, you need to know how much you earn now and how much of it you spend. That means you need a monthly financial statement or a budget. To come up with one, write down everything you spend for a month. That includes your rent, mortgage payment, car payment, utilities, food, and so forth. Then spend a few hours going through your checkbook and credit card bills to find those things you missed, like life insurance premiums, vacations, and gifts.

Expenses come in two categories—fixed and discretionary—but some items fall in both camps: clothing, for instance, and food. There are the basics like underwear and orange juice and there are the luxuries like a cashmere sweaters and caviar.

List your sources of income, then split your expenses into fixed and discretionary and list them here.

Monthly Income

Salary from job	$_____
Receipts from business, consulting	$_____
Investment income	$_____
Rental income	$_____
Total Montly Income	**$_____**

Fixed Expenses

Federal/state taxes	$_____
Social Security taxes	$_____
401(k) plan contribution	$_____
Savings	$_____
Mortgage payment	$_____
Property tax	$_____
Utilities	$_____
Homeowner's insurance	$_____
Telephone	$_____
Rent	$_____

Renter's insurance $_____
Groceries $_____
Clothing $_____
Transportation
  Car payments $_____
  Car insurance $_____
  Gas/maintenance $_____
  Bus, train, subway fare $_____
Life insurance $_____
Disability insurance $_____
Health insurance $_____
Credit card repayments $_____
Personal care (haircuts,
  dry cleaning, etc.) $_____
Total fixed expenses   **$_____**

Discretionary Expenses
Meals out $_____
Movies, video rentals $_____
Cab fare and rental cars $_____
Housecleaning and yard help $_____
Facials, manicures, massage $_____
Entertaining $_____
Clothing $_____
Jewelry $_____
Sports equipment $_____
Vacations $_____
Health club $_____
Charitable contributions $_____
Books, magazines $_____
Gifts $_____
Other $_____
Total discretionary expenses   **$_____**

Total Monthly Expenses   **$_____**

Look at your fixed expenses. This is the amount that you must cover both now and in retirement.

Your Portfolio

REVIEWING AND REPOSITIONING your investment portfolio for retirement—or transition—is a key part of your preparation for change. You have saved throughout your working years. Now you must take stock and see if you have what you need to last the remainder of your lifetime and, if not, what you might do about it.

When you think about your investment portfolio, think about all your assets—everything we've just been talking about in calculation of net worth. That includes your personal residence, a second home if you have one, a family business, the money in all your retirement plans, and the assets you have outside your retirement accounts. Look at the balance sheet you've just prepared as a start.

Your balance sheet provides a list of your assets. But you want to see what your portfolio looks like—or how those assets are grouped by investment category. Roger Gibson, an investment manager in Pittsburgh, has written what many experts consider the bible of asset allocation, *Asset Allocation: Balancing Financial Risk* (McGraw-Hill, 2007), which discusses how diversification limits investing risk. Gibson suggests that you divide your assets into two broad categories. The first is those that produce income such as bonds, money market funds, and Treasury bills. Include here any benefit that you will receive from a traditional pension plan or a defined benefit plan. That represents a fixed income because the monthly benefit is fixed.

The second is investments that represent ownership or equity. That includes stocks, as well as real estate that you own directly, be it your residence, vacation home, or investment property, and any other ownership investments, such as a family business if you have one.

How do you decide how to allocate these assets? William G. Droms, a professor of finance at Georgetown University and a popular speaker on this topic, devised a shorthand method. Value the seven statements below on a scale of 1 to 5, with 1 being "strongly disagree," and 5 being "strongly agree." Then add up your points.

1. I would like to earn a high, long-term total return that will allow my capital to grow faster than the inflation rate; this is one of my most important investment objectives.

2. I would like an investment that provides me with an opportunity to defer taxation of capital gains and/or interest to future years.

3. I do not require a high level of current income from my investments.

4. My major investment goals are relatively long-term.

5. I am willing to tolerate sharp up-and-down swings in the return on my investments in order to seek a higher return than would be expected from more stable investments.

6. I am willing to risk a short-term loss in return for a potentially higher rate of return in the long run.

7. I am financially able to accept a low level of liquidity in my investment portfolio.

Depending on how you scored, here are Droms' recommendations on what percentage of assets to put into each sort of investment.

TOTAL SCORE	money market	fixed income	equities
30 to 35	10	10	80
22 to 29	20	20	60
14 to 21	30	30	40
7 to 13	40	40	20

Financial planners like Droms' test because it acknowledges the different tugs and pulls on investments and comes up with a neat score to determine asset allocation. "It's the best test I've seen," says Harold Evensky, a financial advisor in Coral Gables, Florida.

10

What to Do with Stocks

TRADITIONAL ADVICE TO retirees has been to sell your stocks and buy bonds. Stocks are for young, aggressive investors who have time to let their money grow and who can ride out the bumps. Advisors told retirees that they needed the smoother ride provided by bonds, as well as the income, that they no longer needed growth. Basically, retirees have been told that they are in a phase of life when they can safely consume assets.

Times have changed. Bonds have become nearly as volatile as stocks. But they still hold less return potential than stocks. Retirees need that extra return because many, particularly the elderly, don't have much flexibility in generating earned income. Inflation looms large when earned income stops. And life expectancies have increased so much that retirees cannot safely begin consuming assets when they first retire.

Indeed, the biggest risk in retirement is longevity risk, or the risk that you will outlive your money. Ethan E. Kra, chief actuary for retirement at Mercer and my best source on this issue, has done considerable work on longevity risk. The statistics here belong to his research: The average sixty-five-year-old has no conception of the longevity risk he carries, Kra says. A sixty-five-year-old couple has a one in four chance that one of them will celebrate a ninety-fifth birthday. They have a one in ten chance that one will live to one hundred and beyond.

If you can leave a good chunk of your money in stocks, you should have more money to live on in retirement. We all know what happened to the money in the stock market in 2008 and the first quarter of 2009 and most of us will feel gun-shy of dumping everything into stocks.

Money that you will not need to live on in retirement for five years or more is a good candidate for the stock market. That said, managing stocks when you retire requires substantial time for research on your part or the help of a professional financial advisor. Do not believe that any stock investment is guaranteed. If it were guaranteed, it would not have the potential for higher return. The potential for a high return also means the potential for a high loss.

If we could learn one lesson from the market crash of 2008 and 2009, this should be it: Stock investments are never guaranteed. The experience of target-date funds during the crash is a good example of this. These funds were developed to offer investors—particularly those in 401(k) plans—a diversified investment with a target date such as 2010 and a "glide path" that grows gradually more conservative as the date approaches.

Do investors know that? A survey by Envestnet Asset Management in May 2009 found that only 16 percent of respondents said they had ever heard of target-date funds and 63 percent of those incorrectly described them. The respondents were given a description of the funds to read. After reading it, nearly two-thirds thought they would be able to retire on the fund's target date. The same number believed the funds enabled them to spend less time tracking their progress toward retirement goals. Nearly half said they could stop worrying about investment and savings decisions and leave it to a professional. About 38 percent of respondents believed the funds would produce a guaranteed return. Worse yet, more than one-third believed their money would grow faster in target date funds than in other investments, and nearly 30 percent believed they could save less money with the funds and still meet retirement goals.

What should we make of these survey results? Critics say the funds have not adequately communicated what they are about. But don't we as investors share any of the responsibility? In thirty years of writing about business and investments, I've come across hundreds of investors who were clearly duped. I've also come across hundreds of investors who weren't paying attention. I don't want to let any salesman off the hook. But this is your retirement money! You should not just drift into complacency. The time to find out what you have invested in is now! You should invest in stocks. You should never believe that stocks offer a guarantee of anything. If we could get that one piece of investor information out there, all investors would be much better off.

11

Delay Social Security

ONE OF THE MOST COMMONLY asked questions about Social Security benefits is this: Should I wait until the normal retirement age or start receiving early benefits at age sixty-two? The Social Security Amendments of 1983 made that decision more straightforward because it made benefits "actuarially equivalent," meaning that if you live to the average life expectancy for someone your age, you will receive about the same amount in benefits over your lifetime no matter whether you choose to start receiving benefits at age sixty-two, at full retirement age, at age seventy, or at any age in between.

You would receive a reduced benefit at age sixty-two because you would theoretically be receiving it for a longer period of time. The full benefit is available at full retirement age. But those who continue to delay benefits beyond the full retirement age get credit for the years delayed because they receive a larger benefit at age seventy. After seventy, there is no additional benefit for continuing to delay Social Security.

These amendments gradually raised the full retirement age for those born in 1938 and later until it reaches sixty-six for those born between 1943 and 1954 and sixty-seven for those born in 1960 or later. Early retirement benefits at age sixty-two will decrease as the full retirement age increases, from 80 percent of the full benefit for those born before 1938 to 75 percent of the full benefit for those born from 1943 to 1954 and 70 percent of the full benefit for those born in 1960 or later. The Social Security Administration provides good information at www.ssa.gov on how to calculate benefits as well as factors to consider when you decide your retirement age.

There are a number of sophisticated arguments put forward that compare the appeal of early reduced benefits to later, full benefits.

They rely on life expectancy and the expected rate of return. For example, if you are able to invest your reduced benefit and get a 12 percent return on it, you would come out ahead. Not many Americans today would be willing to make that bet. Likewise, if you live only until age sixty-six, you will clearly come out ahead with the reduced benefit. But because the reduction is based on an "actuarial equivalent," it means that on average workers come out the same financially under each alternative. The amount you receive when you first get benefits sets the base for the amount you will receive the rest of your life although you will receive annual cost-of-living increases. The *New York Times* reported in May 2009 that there will probably not be a cost of living adjustment for 2010.

I certainly don't mean to make light of the decision of when to take Social Security benefits. It is a crucial one. During the Great Recession of the past couple of years, unemployed workers have looked desperately for any possible source of income. And the employment rolls probably won't improve any time soon. *The New York Times* reported on September 27, 2009, that "unemployed Americans now confront a job market that is bleaker than ever in the current recession, and employment prospects are still getting worse."

Job seekers outnumber job openings by six to one, the Times reported, the worst since the government began gathering these statistics in 2000. In July, the most recent data available, the Department of Labor reported that 14.5 million people were unemployed; only 2.4 million full-time permanent jobs were open.[1]

When we are in desperate straits, we do what we have to do. Not if it means robbing a bank of course. But if it means taking government benefits that you are entitled to, that's a different story.

However, for any of us who have any options, I think it's best not to devour retirement benefits while we are still able to work. Ditto for Social Security. Think about some of the factors I've discussed here such as longevity risk and inflation and increasing life expectancies. As much as you can, plan!

---

1. *New York Times,* nytimes.com, http://www.nytimes.com/2009/09/27/business/economy/27jobs.html?ref=todayspaper.

12

Plan for Healthcare

YOU DON'T HAVE to retire at sixty-two, sixty-five, seventy or even eighty. More and more often we hear of someone in her 90s still going into the office every morning. But no matter what age you plan to retire, you will definitely need health care coverage.

Whatever else you do, you must apply for Medicare benefits when you turn sixty five. If you fail to do so, it could cost you more later.

After the recessionary economy, health care, the lack of it, and the Obama Administration's attempts to change the system for delivering it, have consumed more national energy than any other topic in the second half of 2009. And why not? Everyone needs health care. The idea that we might be injured or ill or vulnerable and without anyone to care for us must be a universal fear. Certainly, as we grow older, the fear increases.

Each of us must make plans for our own health care coverage. We can't rely on retiree health care from an employer even if we've been told that we'll get it. All bets are off after the crash of the global economy in 2008. When we watched friends lose their jobs as their employers filed for bankruptcy, we also grew more cynical about the corporate promises made to us.

In an online article for Bankrate.com, Carole Moore wrote in September 2008: "From corporate penthouses to state legislatures, a move to cut and, in some cases eliminate, retiree medical benefits altogether has caught hold. It's leaving upcoming retirees with a dilemma many don't even realize they're facing: How are they going to pay for future medical needs not covered by Medicare? For many, the answer will redefine their retirement."

Moore cites the example of an insurance agent with a 401(k) plan, a pension program and health insurance for himself and his wife who lost all these benefits when his insurance company employer restructured and turned 6,000 agents into "independent agents" rather than company employees. This shift to hire "independent contractors," or self-employed people (like me) who do not receive any employee benefits is a growing one.

For instance, when my daughter graduated from college in May 2009, she could not find a full-time job that offered benefits. Instead, she bought inexpensive health insurance with a high deductible so that she could take on freelance design and photography jobs. The jobs don't pay well. And health insurance is expensive. But I think that this is the wave of the future. Relying on an employer for health insurance is growing more and more risky.

Health care costs are rising at a rate of more than 5 percent per year above inflation. Under law, Medicare insurance premiums must cover 25 percent of the total cost of Medicare. That means that as health care costs continue to go up, so will Medicare premiums.

Moore offers some factors to consider when you think about retiree medical care: For instance, she suggests that you try to find a group plan through a professional or social group.

Don't change jobs until you've checked the health insurance and COBRA benefit you can expect to receive. Congress passed the Consolidated Omnibus Budget Reconciliation Act (COBRA) health benefit provisions in 1986. This law gives employees the right to continue their medical insurance under the employer's group plan when they leave a job, albeit at a higher cost. The COBRA benefits were substantially improved in the Obama budget stimulus bill.

Beyond that, there's all the tried and true advice: Begin living a healthier lifestyle. Get preventive medicine and annul physicals and routine tests. Exercise to stay fit. And consider delaying retirement.

To learn more on reasons baby boomers should stay alert, stay active, keep learning, keeping earning and stay alive, I recommend James Walker and Linda Lewis's book, *Work Wanted* (Wharton School Publishing, 2009). Whatever your age, start thinking and planning for how you will take control of managing these life transitions.

So many Americans have been thrown out of work and have lost their health insurance during the Great Recession. They've been force to act out of desperation. Those who still have time to plan, must get going.

PART SIX

STEPS TO TAKE IN RETIREMENT

Once More with Confidence

Visit any bookstore or newsstand, and you'll see dozens of magazine stories and books on saving for retirement: How to save a million dollars by age fifty. There is no shortage of information on how much you should save and where to invest it. Investing has long been the glamour girl of financial planning.

But what will happen to all those books and magazines now that so many Americans feel burned by the advice? Can any of us read an article titled "Seven Safe Stocks to Buy Now," and keep a straight face? Is there anyone who survived the market meltdown of 2008 and 2009 without serious dents in a once prosperous portfolio? The 2009 American Retirement Study by Scottrade found that just 32 percent of Americans believe they will ever be able to fully retire. That's down from 39 percent in 2008.

That's one task of this book: to help investors pick themselves up and invest again with confidence. Equally important for a book on retirement accounts is providing advice on how to pull that money out in retirement and how to stretch it out, if possible.

Lump Sums

WHEN YOU RETIRE with a lump sum of money in your 401(k) plan, it belongs to you. Whether it is $20,000 or $1.4 million, you are entitled to take it home with you. If you take it out of your 401(k) account and deposit it in the bank, though, or, worse yet, spend it, you will owe taxes on all of it. Remember when we talked about the government's role in 401(k) plans? This is what the government has been waiting for: The Internal Revenue Service (IRS) gets the payoff for all those years of tax deferral when you take the money out. You have control over when that tax hit will happen. If you take a lump sum of $1 million, roughly one-third to one-half of that money will go to taxes.

This is what you do not want to do. What are your other options? Some taxpayers may want to consider leaving the money with their employer, which I will discuss in the following section. But most taxpayers will probably want to roll their 401(k) money over into an Individual Retirement Account. This preserves the tax-deferred status of the money until you begin making mandatory withdrawals from the account at age 70½.

Advisors typically tell plan participants not to combine the rollover money with traditional Individual Retirement Account (IRA) money because the traditional money would "taint" the 401(k) money so that it could no longer be rolled into another qualified plan at another employer. Instead, you should use a separate IRA, called a "conduit IRA," for the money from the qualified plan. That's because the government has sometimes taken the position that you cannot roll over non-qualified funds to a new employer. Although this rule is not as firm as it once was, the best advice is still to keep the employer money separate. We never know when the rules might change and it's always best to be flexible.

One advantage of putting it in an IRA is that the money is no longer off-limits to you. You cannot borrow money from an IRA. But if you are over 59½, you can tap into the money whenever you like, paying tax on it as you withdraw it. For many Americans, the chunk of money from their retirement plan represents the biggest asset they have. If that describes your situation, and you have little investing experience, either do some research or get some help.

By help I mean a good, independent financial advisor who will take your entire financial situation into account before dispensing advice, not a stock or bond or insurance salesman. The fact that baby boomers are rolling over big 401(k) account balances as they retire or leave their jobs is not a secret in the financial community. Expect to have people preying on you and your money. I would not accept advice from anyone who contacted me from a list of retiring employees and offered "help" with important money decisions. What you do not need at this point is a Bernie Madoff, the "investment guru" whom I discussed at the beginning of the book who admitted that he lost billions of investors' dollars because he never even invested them but rather spent them or sent them off as returns to other investors.

Investing the money yourself is possible. You need three things. First, you need an asset-allocation model. That's a plan for how you will split your money between different types of investments like stocks, bonds, and cash. Second, you need to choose individual securities or exchange-traded funds (ETFs) or mutual funds to build your portfolio. And third, you need the discipline to sit tight through thick and thin.

The best way to fritter away your life savings is by tinkering with your investment mix every time you read a newspaper or magazine story or investment advice on the Internet. If you plan to invest on your own, you need some kind of model such as those provided by www.morningstar.com, www.financialengines.com, or numerous other financial planning Web sites.

Many of the target-date funds discussed earlier in the book were designed to do this management job for you, shifting assets to more conservative investments as you age. The evolving investment mix is referred to as the *glide path* of that fund. If you've been happy with the performance of your target-date fund, you may wish to do more research on it and see what its objectives are and whether it might suit you in this transition phase of your life. If a target-date fund is well and carefully managed, it can provide you with a managed portfolio in one fund. Many experts I interviewed—such as Ted Benna, the father of the 401(k) plan—believe that the target-date funds of the future will provide the best option for many investors. John Cammack, head of third-party distribution at T. Rowe Price, tells me that many companies that offer target-date funds allow the plan participant to leave the money in the fund to continue to grow and be managed during retirement.

Leaving the Money Where It Is

MOST EMPLOYEES take their 401(k) money with them when they leave or retire from their employer. But it's not always the best move. There are some compelling reasons to leave your retirement money with your former employer, at least for the time being. For instance, you may have special investment options that you can't duplicate outside the plan, such as a target-date fund, or your employer may subsidize the plan in some way so that investing costs less for you and your co-workers.

Qualified plans, which include the 401(k) plan, sometimes have legal advantages over individual retirement accounts (IRAs), too. For example, the money in a qualified plan cannot be tapped by your creditors if you declare bankruptcy. (It's also safe in the event of your company's bankruptcy.) But IRA money typically can. Money in qualified plans is also eligible for more favorable tax treatments such as forward averaging. When Congress makes new rules about retirement plans, they typically apply to qualified plans but not to IRAs.

So you shouldn't automatically decide to take the money with you. Do some checking first. Find out what happens if you leave it in the plan. The basic guideline is this: If you have less than $5,000 in your 401(k) account, your employer is permitted to write you a check to cash you out of the plan and end the administrative fees associated with your account. If you have more than $5,000, your employer must permit you to remain in the plan. If you have less than $5,000, you should ask your employer to roll the balance over to an IRA rather than writing a check to you. Or you can contact the vendor you want to use for your IRA and ask that company to arrange for the rollover.

Pay attention to your employer's attitude toward you and your 401(k) money. As you know by now, employers began using 401(k) plans to shift the responsibility for retirement investing to employees. Some are eager to be done with it. They really don't want you in the plan for any longer than necessary. Look for signs of this attitude in the 401(k) materials your employer furnishes. Other employers want retirees to stay to help pay the bills. Retirees require fewer services than active employees, yet they have higher account balances. So if the plan fees are based on a percent of assets, the retirees subsidize the active employees.

Another group of employers feels very responsible for employees' retirement goals. This group may provide special enticements to keep employees in the plan so that the company knows their money is still protected in retirement. When I wrote the original version of this book, I heard about what Albany International Corporation, a supplier to the paper industry based in Albany, New York, did to assist its employees. The company permitted employees to put all or part of their 401(k) balances into the company pension plan and receive it in monthly payouts as a supplement to regular pension income. That allowed employees to get professional money management by a pension expert and a steady stream of income. I find it encouraging that some employers are reaching out to their 401(k) participants and giving them sound options on what to do with their money at retirement rather than just sending them off adrift with a huge lump sum.

This monthly payout plan resembles an annuity purchased from an insurance company with a couple of important differences. Unlike an insurer, Albany International offered the plan at no cost to employees. Buying an annuity with similar features would be expensive. Mercer, the benefits consultant that designed the plan for Albany International, surveyed the annuity market to see how the plan stacked up. Albany International's return on its defined benefit plan was about 18 percent better than the best annuity they could find because there was no sales commission and no fees attached to the company's plan.

This plan provides a nice example of a company doing something extra for employees and taking on some responsibility for their lives in retirement. You shouldn't expect your employer to be so generous. But if the employer is, you certainly want to find out about it. Too often in today's work world we see employee and employer pitted against one another right down to the last nickel. That's too bad.

When you get close to retirement—or to leaving your employer— schedule an interview with your human resources department. Check the resources available to you online. Talk, too, with recent retirees and try to get a sense of how they made their decisions about their 401(k) money and of how they were treated by the company in the plan once they retired. And go back to the documents you've received from the plan to look at the plan's expenses.

Convert to Roth?

THE ROTH RETIREMENT ACCOUNT, named for its sponsor, William B. Roth Jr., a U.S. senator from Delaware, has many advantages over traditional Individual Retirement Accounts (IRAs) and 401(k) plans. However, many Americans have not been able to use it because of income limitations. For 2009, eligibility to contribute to a Roth IRA phases out between $105,000 and $120,000 for single filers and $166,000 to $176,000 for those married and filing jointly Further, in 2009, only those taxpayers who earned less than $100,000, either as a single or a couple, same limit, could convert pre-tax IRA money to a Roth. But there is big news in the Roth family for taxpayers. Beginning in 2006, employers were authorized to add an option to 401(k) plans to permit them to take Roth (after-tax) contributions, which allows employees to set aside a much larger amount of after-tax money for retirement. And in 2010, the income ceiling for converting from the traditional to Roth IRA disappears.

The Roth is something of a backwards IRA or 401(k) account. With the Roth, you contribute dollars that have already been taxed, rather than pre-tax dollars. But these dollars will never be taxed again. You can take them out tax-free even before you turn 59½, provided you have been in the plan for five years and you withdraw principal rather than earnings. There is no 10 percent penalty for these early withdrawals.

Equally important, there is no mandatory withdrawal schedule for the Roth. You pay tax on the money before it goes into your account, and from that time on, principal and earnings are tax free. If you live to be eighty or ninety or older, you don't have to take anything out of the account. And you can continue to contribute to the Roth as long as you keep working, whereas with the regular IRA, you cannot contribute to after age 70½.

The ability to delay withdrawals and to continue adding to the Roth after age 70½ are what make it appealing to me. Like a lot of people, I plan to continue working as long as I can; my main worry is that I will outlive my money, which wouldn't take very long to do at this point. So the ability to continue to contribute and not be forced to take withdrawals at any particular time looks to me like a big plus. Although you must pay tax on the money before you set it aside, I think this flexibility in retirement is worth it.

Beginning in 2010, the income ceiling for converting to a Roth will be removed, but the catch is that you will have to pay tax on the money when you convert it. Although that sounds harsh to those of us who have already watched our retirement portfolios shrink, there are reasons to consider converting. This could be a good year to convert, partly because of the market crash of 2008 and the 2009 market doldrums. With portfolio balances shrunken, we may be paying tax on less money. Hopefully the markets will bounce back, and then we'll get the boost in an after-tax Roth account.

With talk of rising tax rates to pay for the huge budget deficits, you may be in a higher tax bracket when you retire than you are now. In that case, converting to a Roth now makes sense. Those who convert in 2010 have another advantage: They are permitted to split the tax bill in half and pay one half in 2011 and the other half in 2012.

One other note on the Roth 401(k): The contribution limits go for both pre-tax and after-tax money. So for 2009, you can contribute both pre-tax and after-tax money, but you cannot contribute more than $16,500 in total, or $22,000 if you are older than fifty. And the employer match continues to go in pre-tax.

These Roth account rules are still new and complicated. If you have a traditional IRA that you want to convert to a Roth in 2010, do some research or get some advice. If you have a chance to contribute to a Roth 401(k), I think you should seriously consider it.

Required Distributions

YOU MUST BEGIN taking money from tax-deferred retirement accounts, which include individual retirement accounts (IRAs) and 401(k) plans, but not Roth accounts, by April 1 of the year following the calendar year in which you turn 70½, unless you are still working. If you are a participant in a qualified plan, like a 401(k) plan, and you are still working, you may postpone withdrawals. But even if you care still working, you must start taking distributions if you own more than 5 percent of the company.

Ten years ago, the rules for required minimum distributions were so complex and arcane that dozens of consultants earned a living by providing the best advice to clients. And many of those who did not get expert advice simply got a rotten deal. But in 2001 the IRS simplified the rules, and they are much more straightforward and easy to apply today. Still, this is a crucial issue and you must take great care to do it properly. The necessary instructions are available on live at www.irs.gov.

When a taxpayer reaches the minimum distribution age of 70½, he has until April 1 of the following year to take the first required minimum distribution from his plan. However, the second distribution will be due by December 31 of that same year. For that reason, some taxpayers decide to take the first distribution a year earlier than necessary rather than waiting and being forced to take two distributions (and pay tax on them) in the same year.

Most taxpayers will use the uniform lifetime table to figure the required minimum distributions (RMD). This table can be found on the Internal Revenue Service (IRS) Web site (www.irs.gov). It provides a bit more generous table or, in other words, it allows the taxpayer to take less out of the account than the earlier rules. Of course, you can always take more out of the account than what is required. If you do not take a distribution or if your distribution is not at least equal to the required minimum distribution, you may owe a 50 percent excise tax on the amount not distributed as required.

The distribution amount changes from year to year because life expectancy is reduced every year you grow older, but not by a full year. Your minimum distribution is calculated by dividing the value of the account at year end by the distribution period in the IRS table.

Suppose you plan to take a RMD in 2010. You will need to know your account balance as of December 31, 2009. You also need to know your distribution amount based on the uniform lifetime table. For example, if you will be seventy-two in 2010, the distribution period is 25.6 years. Suppose your account balance on December 31, 2009 is $100,000. You divide $100,000 by 25.6 to see that your required distribution is $3,906. The following year you will need to go back to the table to get your new life expectancy.

If your spouse is more than ten years younger than you, use the joint life expectancy table, which will allow you to take a smaller pay-out. If an IRA accountholder dies, the spouse can roll over the money to his or her own account and follow the same rules. If the beneficiary is an inheritor who is not the spouse, the payout is calculated based on the inheritor's age plus one year. So if a forty-year-old grandchild inherits money, her age the following year (forty-one), would allow a payout of 42.7 years. Rules for calculating the required minimum distributions are the same for IRAs and 401(k)s.

However, if an IRA account holder has several different accounts he must calculate the required distribution from each one. But he is permitted to take the total required distribution from one account. That is also true for 403 (b) plans. Required distributions from other retirement plans such as 401(k) and 457 plans must be withdrawn separately from each account.

Longevity Risk

WE'VE DISCUSSED how to take money out of your plan in retirement, but we haven't talked about how to make certain that you have enough money in your plan to last the rest of your life. Indeed, as I mentioned earlier, the biggest risk in retirement is longevity risk, or the risk that you will outlive your money. Not surprisingly, financial adivsers do a good deal of work in this area. William P. Bengen a financial advisor in El Cajon, California is considered expert in doing research on "sustainable withdrawals" or taking withdrawals that will sustain your portfolio rather then devour it. His book, *Conserving Client Portfolios During Retirement* is available at amazon.com or through his Web site www.billbengen.com. Ethan E. Kra, chief actuary for retirement at Mercer, has done considerable work on longevity risk, as discussed in detail in Part Five, page 196. Not only are the chances for an extremely long life good, but as people pass the age of eighty-five, their ability to manage their finances decreases. Expecting them to take charge of their affairs is un-realistic. "We're asking people to do something they're not capable of doing," Kra says.

His solution: Longevity insurance in the form of an annuity that starts paying at age eighty-five and pays for life. He suggests that at age sixty, a person take 10 percent of the money from his 401(k) plan or individual retirement account (IRA), go to an insurance company, and buy an annuity that spreads the money across the risk pool and starts paying out at age eighty-five.

The taxpayer keeps the other 90 percent of the money and spends it down over his life expectancy, as I've discussed in this book. There is no provision yet for a taxpayer to take the money out of an IRA or 401(k) account and buy the annuity with pre-tax dollars, Kra says, but that might happen. "That would require an act of

Congress," he said. "They're looking at it." At least two life insurance companies have such a product in development.

Annuities have been around for decades and they've long played a role in spreading assets out over a lifetime. The trouble is, not everyone has enough money to buy an annuity that can pay enough to live on over a 100-year life expectancy. That's where this product is different. This longevity product has a special annuity feature, Kra says. "It doesn't pay anything to those who die." So anyone who buys an annuity at age sixty-five and dies before eighty-five gets nothing. That means the product carries less selection against the insurance company and therefore pays out two to three times what you would expect to get for a life annuity. There is no cost for insurance. Let me put this in another way: With most insurance products, company underwriters must try to determine how many people will collect benefits from a policy and price it accordingly. For this product, only those who live past age eighty-five will receive benefits. That makes if a straightforward underwriting task. I believe this is a great product for certain people because it is a true spreading of risk. Half the people who buy the annuity will die before it pays out. The people who buy it do not know whether they will need it. "This is for the person who has enough money to last until life expectancy," Kra says. "For them, it offers inflation protection." I recently visited friends who have a large disparity in age. He is seventy-two. She is fifty-four. They felt that this might be just the right product to protect her in later years as she has no family and they have no children together.

I still see a problem in persuading people to spend money on a product that might never result in a payoff. Americans typically want a payoff. Yet, most good insurance is precisely that: a spreading of the risk. When you buy fire or auto insurance, you hope you will never need to use it. I see this life annuity as a similar product. My experience with Kra over the years has taught me that most of his ideas eventually become law in one form or another, and I've never known him to have a bad idea. For me, the problem will be to come up with the premium at age sixty-five.

PART SEVEN

RETIREMENT PLANS BY OTHER NAMES

401(k) Plan Alternatives

Over the past thirty years, "401(k)" has become a household word, even a cocktail party topic. These plans have turned Americans who had never heard of a mutual fund into investors who hold conversations on the relative merits of target-date funds versus emerging-market funds versus large-cap growth.

What should you do, then, if you do not have a 401(k) plan? Millions of Americans do not have any kind of retirement plan at work. Millions more work for themselves and have some type of individual plan. Another huge group of Americans qualify for salary reduction plans at work that are similar to a 401(k) plan but with slightly different provisions. Most of these plans pre-date 401(k) accounts. They are called 403(b) plans, 457 plans, or sometimes TDAs or "tax-deferred annuities."

Such alternatives bear enough resemblance to 401(k) plans to make many of the general rules of thumb worth knowing, particularly those in the investment area. Many 403(b) plans at hospitals, for example, offer the same broad range of investment options that you would expect to find in a good 401(k) plan. Yet these plans have some quirky differences that require some extra work on your part if you are to get the most out of them.

Here are some of the things you should look into if you work at a nonprofit such as a hospital, a school, a charitable foundation, a government agency, or some other employer that uses a salary reduction plan other than a 401(k) plan.

403(b) Plans

MILLIONS OF AMERICANS who work for nonprofits and government agencies have a salary reduction plan at work that is similar to—yet different from—a 401(k) plan. These school teachers, college professors, doctors, nurses, and government employees are permitted to contribute to a 403(b) plan, authorized by a different section of the Internal Revenue Code.

Section 403(b) was added to the Internal Revenue Code in 1958, a full twenty years before section 401(k), to permit employees at nonprofits and government agencies to set aside pre-tax money in an annuity contract offered by an insurance company. Thanks to its roots in the insurance industry, the 403(b) plan is often referred to as a TDA or "tax-deferred annuity."

In 1974, Congress added paragraph 7 to section 403(b). This newer provision permits employees to set up their retirement plans with mutual fund companies instead of insurance companies. Today participants in 403(b) plans can choose between annuities and mutual funds, but they cannot choose other options permitted in a 401(k) plan, such as guaranteed investment contracts (GICs) and individual stocks.

Participants in a 403(b) are permitted to contribute $16,500 for 2009 to their 403(b) account, just as they would with a 401(k) plan. Participants older than fifty are allowed to contribute $22,000. The 403(b) plan also has a catch-up provision that entitles participants to contribute extra money for five years. I spent a great deal of time trying to understand this catch-up provision so that I could explain it, but I could not find anyone who understood it well enough to explain it to me in plain English. Here is the best advice I can give you: If you have not contributed to a 403(b) plan when you were entitled to do so, or have contributed less than the maximum amount and now have extra money that you would like to contribute, get the advice of an accountant on how to calculate catch-up contributions.

The pension simplification rules that were tacked on to the minimum-wage bill passed in July 1996 provided that all nonprofits and government agencies would be permitted to set up 401(k) plans if they choose, but that hasn't happened, chiefly because of the cost of setting up a new plan.

Meanwhile, there have been big changes in the 403(b) plans, effective January 1, 2009, that will make these plans more similar to the 401(k) plan. Critics hope the new rules will eliminate some of the flaws in the old plans. For example, some employers took no role in the 403(b) plans at all, allowing insurance company salesmen to roam the hallways and school lunchrooms and give seminars to recruit school employees. Some of these marketers provided terrible and excessively expensive products. Some sold rigidly structured annuities that collected savings during working years and then converted—with no other option for the employee—into a high-cost payout annuity. In short, no one was minding the store, and employees paid for it. Hopefully those days are behind us.

Still, if you have a 403 (b) plan, pay attention to investing options. Do not allow yourself to be "sold" a plan by a fast-talking salesperson. So many people became incredibly disappointed with their retirement plans after the 2008 calendar year. If you are one of them, the best lesson you could learn is that you must become more involved. That doesn't mean you should be spinning investments like a roulette wheel. It does mean you should be paying attention. Do some research on market benchmarks like the Standard & Poor's 500 Stock Market Index and the Lehman Brothers aggregate bond market index. (This has nothing to do with the performance of Lehman Brothers. It is simply an index complied by Lehman Brothers over the years and now marketed by Barclay's.) You want some measure to compare your portfolio to the overall market. Better yet, set up an online portfolio at a site like aol.com or bloomberg.com so you can monitor it.

2

ERISA or No?

THROUGHOUT THIS BOOK, we've discussed various pieces of pension legislation that affect pensions paid to America's workers. The granddaddy of them is the Employee Retirement Income Security Act of 1974 (ERISA). ERISA requires that employers be prudent and vigilant in selecting, maintaining and reviewing retirement plan investments. All 401(k) plans are governed by ERISA. But employers who sponsor 403(b) plans have a choice about whether or not to comply with ERISA. About half do so. Employees who participate in non-ERISA plans must do more work to make certain they choose a good plan and make good investment choices.

An employer that sponsors an ERISA plan chooses a vendor for a 403(b) plan in much the same way as 401(k) plan sponsors do. Mercer's Ethan E. Kra refers to the 403(b) ERISA plan as a plan with a capital P because the employer takes charge of the plan. Even government employers, who are exempt from ERISA, can put together this type of plan. The employer provides educational materials like those offered in a 401(k) plan as well as a summary plan description. The employer may provide a matching contribution. And the employer must file form 5500, which is an annual form that must be sent to the Internal Revenue Service (IRS) for every qualified plan.

Many other employers leave it entirely up to employees to decide whether or how they will invest their 403(b) money. These employers simply agree to withhold the money from your salary and to send it to the investment company of your choice. They have no responsibility for the choice you make. In fact, they may, and probably will, allow salesmen to solicit your business without screening these people. And then they will send the money wherever the employee wants it to go. Kra calls this a plan with a lowercase p because it has few boundaries, and the employer has few responsibilities.

The good news is that many plan participants are becoming involved in monitoring the 403 (b) plans, some of them online. For instance, take a look at 403(b)wise.com for some solid information about your plan.

Kra's wife, for example, worked in a private school where she was told she could invest retirement money wherever she liked, provided she collected and filled out the forms and turned them in. "The employer has no responsibility other than forwarding the payroll deduction and filling out the W-2 properly," Kra says.

From the employer's point of view, the non-ERISA plan can be very appealing because there are no responsibilities, fiduciary or otherwise. But from your perspective as the employee, this type of plan is appealing only if you know a fair amount about both investing and retirement vehicles. The plans in this category fit the old saw about insurance policies: These 403(b) plans are sold, not bought. The same insurance agents who push life insurance policies call teachers and others who qualify for 403(b) plans and try to sell them an annuity product, usually without laying out the pros and cons.

I've talked with dozens of people who bought these plans—many of them teachers—without knowing what they'd purchased. Most simply referred to their plan as a TDA. That is a recipe for disaster. If your employer is not involved in monitoring your plan, you must monitor it yourself.

Because many of the 403(b) products have surrender charges, it is critical to decide which type of product you want before you buy it. Be careful, too, that you check the various provisions of the agreement you sign. Many of the annuity products lock you in for life. Once you buy the annuity, you must use it to accumulate your retirement money and then, once retired, you must accept the terms of that company's annuity payout.

Check these provisions before you start contributing to a 403(b) plan. If you already have a plan and discover that its terms are unattractive, be sure to look at the surrender fee before you decide to get out of the plan.

403(b) Plan Reform

ONE OF THE PROBLEMS with 403(b) plans is the overwhelming percent of plan assets that are in high-fee, insurance-based products. In 2006, nearly 80 percent of the $652 billion dollars invested in 403(b) plans was held in annuity products, a high-fee choice that is not particularly suitable for retirement plans. Indeed, today it is widely accepted among financial professionals that putting an annuity inside a retirement account is a bad idea. That's because an annuity provides one layer of tax deferral, at a cost, and a retirement account provides another. Yet the basic 403(b) plan does exactly that.

In 1974, Congress added paragraph 7 to section 403(b), permitting employees to set up their retirement plans with mutual fund companies instead of insurance companies. Either company's products might include mutual funds as an investment option but the insurance company product wraps an annuity around the mutual funds at an additional cost, according to Mercer's Ethan E. Kra. Mutual funds come in two varieties—those with commissions and those without commissions. But all annuities have some kind of load or commission. "The load may be buried inside the annuity interest rate," Kra says. "But it's there."

The good news here is that a sweeping reform of 403(b) plans to address these abuses became effective on January 1, 2009. The Treasury Department and the Internal Revenue Service (IRS) released final regulations in 2008 designed to diminish or eliminate differences between the 403(b) plan and the 401(k) plan. These regulations are the first comprehensive set of new regulations to section 403(b) since 1964.

The new regulations require that all plans create a plan document spelling out the rules of the plan and that they give employees access to this document. The employer must regularly notify all eligible employees of their ability to participate in the plan. Employees must be allowed to transfer plan assets to a different vendor either inside or outside of the plan as well as to roll over the money to an IRA.

The new regulations could do much to guide 403(b) plan sponsors to operate in the interest of plan participants to provide them with retirement plan benefits with transparent and reasonable costs. One critic, W. Scott Simon, who wrote a model plan for 403(b) plans that was published in the November 2007 issue of *Morningstar Advisor*, suggests that 403(b) plans should simply get rid of annuities, the insurance company investment options that run to 200 to 500 basis points in expenses.

Simon also suggests that when a plan does offer mutual funds as an investment option for 403(b) plans, the school officials should include no more than ten to twelve individual funds, each low cost, broadly diversified, and significantly different from the other funds. "An exhausting array of studies has shown that the more choices (of anything) people are given, the less confident they are in their selections—if they even make them," Simon writes.

This is only the beginning of a big change for 403(b) plans. A good place to keep up on these reforms and all other issues affecting 403(b) plans is www.403bwise.com.

I find it very positive that more attention is being focused on retirement plans other than the 401(k), which is the glamour girl of retirement plans, thanks to all the plan sponsors who offer it. But, going forward, we all need to focus on what's best in our retirement plan and how to capitalize on it, as well as what's not so good and how to make the best of it.

Resources

Wherever you are in your career, make your 401(k) plan the core of your investment portfolio. Do you have an investment portfolio? Can you describe what's in it? To many people the word "portfolio" itself is intimidating. All it really means, though, is a collection of assets—securities and other investments such as bonds, gold, art, and real estate. Build your portfolio in a coherent way with your 401(k) plan as the centerfold.

You probably own some investments. You may own a home. Perhaps you have some mutual funds. Or maybe you've invested money in one of your passions, like Inuit art or tribal instruments. These various assets and investments represent part of your balance sheet, but a true investment portfolio should be more than just a list of investments. Some thought should be given to how these investments fit together and work together as a team.

Unfortunately, most people don't spend enough time on that part. They buy mutual funds, stocks, and other investments haphazardly, based on tips from friends or recommendations from brokers. If they get a year-end bonus, they buy a fund, or perhaps they take a vacation! If it's April 15 and individual retirement account (IRA) contribution time, they buy another fund. Then they read that a hot fund is about to close to new members, and they buy it—to get in under the wire, which is usually a mistake in any case. What they end up with is a grabbag. How it will perform is anybody's guess. My guess is that it will be disappointing.

To make the most of your money—and your life—you need a plan. One simple way to get one is to go to an independent financial advisor and pay to get one set up. Or you could take advantage of all the resources and educational materials offered by your employer and work one out yourself. Keep it simple. In the first edition of this book, we included sample portfolios for various investment strategies. But we're not going to do that this time. Markets have changed and so have the investment options in 401(k) plans. Furthermore, investment goals are extremely diverse. Pre-packaged investment plans based on simple raw data (current age, assets, retirement age, risk profile, etc.) do not take into consideration the many complicated and variable factors that influence proper planning. A detailed portfolio that shows 2 percent of this and 8 percent of that is no longer realistic for 401(k) plan participants, if it ever was.

You may have a target-date fund or lifecycle fund available in your plan that is offered as a complete portfolio in one fund. If so, check it out. The 2010 target-date funds are the first to come to maturity. Even though many 2010 target-date funds turned in disappointing results for 2008, most experts I talked with believe the idea of the target-date fund is still a sound one and that sponsors will tinker with the funds to make them better after this initial experience. Many large 401(k) plan sponsors are assembling a mix of the investments in their plans and offering them as a package, according to Pam Hess, director of retirement research at Hewitt Associates in Lincolnshire, Illinois. In addition, consultants are often willing to take fiduciary responsibility for setting up the fund's "glide path," or the changing asset mix over time.

One of the big issues in target-date funds is this: What happens at the target date? How should the assets be allocated during the accumulation phase, and how should the glide path operate? Ron Surz, managing director of Target-Date Analytics, who has done a good deal of research on target-date indexes, argues that the target date is the end of the accumulation phase, which likely occurs when the investor retires. At that point, Surz says, the 401(k) plan participant can be expected to take her money out of the plan and set up a new asset allocation for the distribution phase. "No fund can apply to both stages, the accumulation and distribution phase," he says. Surz sets up his target dates to be used in the accumulating phase. Surz is a knowledgeable and active player in this market. For his view of the funds, see www.tdbench.com.

Many of the mutual fund companies have designed their target-date funds as a lifetime investment. That means the accumulation phase continues to the target date, which is the age the participant retires. But the portfolio continues to be managed for life for this investor and carries him through the distribution phase. You will want to know which type of target-date fund is offered in your 401(k) plan. Because this is one of the hottest topics in this market place, you should expect your employer to provide clarity on the way your plan's funds operate.

Much other 401(k) plan information can be found online. Start with your own company's Web site or the Web site of the plan's vendor to get a better understanding. Because Americans were blindsided by economic events in 2008 and 2009, most plan sponsors are eager to provide information and to answer questions about their plans.

Many other investing sites are available online. Below are resources you might check for other types of information about life's challenges and transitions and how you might make the most of them.

■ Gerri Detweiler is one of the country's top credit specialists. She serves as Credit Advisor for Credit.com, a free Web site offering a wealth of tools to help consumers improve their financial lives. In addition to co-authoring *Debt Collection Answers,* she is the co-author of *Reduce Debt, Reduce Stress* (Good Advice Press, 2009), *The Ultimate Credit Handbook* (in print since 1993 and named one of the top five personal finance books of the year by *Money* magazine), and co-author of *Invest In Yourself: Six Secrets to a Rich Life* and *Slash Your Debt, Save Money & Secure Your Future.* If debt is part of your problem, I recommend Detweiler's work.

■ Tara Brach is author of *Radical Acceptance—Embracing Your Life with the Heart of a Buddha* (Bantam, 2004). You might think this is a little far fetched for 401(k) investors. True, it's more about your life than your money. But that's good. This book is recommended by Marjorie A. Burnett, a registered life planner who says she uses it to better understand her life and her clients and to better communicate to pursue and achieve their life purposes.

■ Sara Lawrence-Lightfoot, a Harvard professor and sociologist, interviewed men and woman older than fifty across the country who have changed their lives. She writes about them in *The Third Chapter: Passion, Risk and Adventure in the 25 years after 50* (Farrar, Straus and Giroux, 2009).

■ For information on transitions, see *Work Wanted: Protect Your Retirement Plans in Uncertain Times* by James W. Walker and Linda H. Lewis (Wharton School Publishing, 2009).

■ The Web site 403bwise.com is a great source for participants of 403(b) plans.

■ There are a couple of sites that help job seekers older than fifty: GoliathJobs.com amd JobsOver50.com. to name two. In addition, the networking site, Linkedin.com, is becoming a popular resource.

■ Lifetwo.com is a Web site about mid-life improvement, with visitors from 210 countries with about 70 percent from the United States.

Index

About the Author

Mary Rowland has been a journalist for thirty years, a half dozen of them as weekly columnist for the Sunday *New York Times*. She is news editor for the Web site advisors4advisors.com, a site for financial services professionals. Her articles and essays have appeared in *Fortune, BusinessWeek, USA Today, Ladie's Home Journal, Family Circle, Women's Day*, and many other publications. She speaks regularly about money and values and co-hosted a weekly national radio call-in show about investing and personal finance. Rowland received a master of fine arts in fiction writing from Vermont College in 2002 and studies theology at Bard College in Annandale-on-Hudson, NY. She has a B.A. and M.A. in Russian history. Rowland lives in New York's Hudson Valley with her husband, Bob Casey. They have two grown children.

About Bloomberg

Bloomberg L.P., founded in 1981, is a global information services, news, and media company. Headquartered in New York, the company has sales and news operations worldwide.

Serving customers on six continents, Bloomberg, through its wholly-owned subsidiary Bloomberg Finance L.P., holds a unique position within the financial services industry by providing an unparalleled range of features in a single package known as the Bloomberg Professional® service. By addressing the demand for investment performance and efficiency through an exceptional combination of information, analytic, electronic trading, and straight-through-processing tools, Bloomberg has built a worldwide customer base of corporations, issuers, financial intermediaries, and institutional investors.

Bloomberg News, founded in 1990, provides stories and columns on business, general news, politics, and sports to leading newspapers and magazines throughout the world. Bloomberg Television, a 24-hour business and financial news network, is produced and distributed globally in seven languages. Bloomberg Radio is an international radio network anchored by flagship station Bloomberg 1130 (WBBR-AM) in New York.

In addition to the Bloomberg Press line of books, Bloomberg publishes *Bloomberg Markets* magazine. To learn more about Bloomberg, call a sales representative at:

London: +44-20-7330-7500
New York: +1-212-318-2000
Tokyo: +81-3-3201-8900